A Short History of India

Pocket Essentials by Gordon Kerr

A Short History of India

GORDON KERR

POCKET ESSENTIALS

First published in 2017 by
Pocket Essentials, an imprint of
Oldcastle Books Ltd, PO Box 394,
Harpenden, Herts, AL5 1XJ
www.pocketessentials.com

Editor: Nick Rennison

A CIP catalogue record for this book is available from the British Library.

ISBN
978-1-84344-922-5 (Print)
978-1-84344-923-2 (epub)
978-1-84344-924-9 (Kindle)
978-1-84344-925-6 (PDF)

2 4 6 8 10 9 7 5 3 1

Typeset by Avocet Typeset, Somerton, Somerset TA11 6RT
in 12.4pt Perpetua

Printed and bound in Great Britain by Clays Ltd, St Ives plc

For John Kumria

CONTENTS

Introduction

India takes its name from the word 'Sindhu', the Sanskrit name for the great river, the Indus that flows for almost two thousand miles from the Himalayas to the Arabian Sea. It became 'Hindu' in the pronunciation of the Persians and came to stand for not just the river but also for the people who lived beyond its eastern bank. It evolved into 'Indu' and later into the English name for the country 'India'.

Not only did this mighty river give the country its name, it was also the birthplace of Indian civilisation, and a mysterious culture developed along its banks more than five millennia ago. Not much is known about this culture and its customs but in the centuries following its decline, India's vast history began to be played out, notions of statehood and monarchy developed and small kingdoms and large empires came and went with the shifting sands of time. Empires such as the Maurya whose most successful emperor, Ashoka – one of the most important figures in all Indian history – ruled almost the entire subcontinent in the middle of the third century BC. India has always been subject to incursions from beyond its borders and, following the decline of Ashoka's empire, it suffered a series of invasions from Europe and from Central Asia. Large parts of the modern country of India were ruled by Indo-Scythians, Indo-Parthians, Kushans and Indo-Greeks, all of whom left their mark on what was a diverse collection of races and ethnicities populating the land.

Another great empire, the Guptas created something of a golden age in India, bringing a period of peace, prosperity and achievement from the fourth to the middle of the sixth century AD. Under great rulers such as Chandragupta I, Samudragupta, and Chandragupta II, there were exciting discoveries in science, technology, engineering, art, literature and mathematics, and developments in religious thought and philosophy contributed to the development of Hindu culture.

The Guptas were followed by other dynasties such as the Chalukyas, the Pallavas and the Pandyas, all of which contributed to India's rich and fascinating past. Outside forces still played their part, however, and invaders from Central Asia from the tenth to twelfth centuries established the Delhi Sultanate which brought India together again under one centralised rule. By 1526, the Mughals had moved in and ruled large parts of the country. Mughal decline led to Maratha power in the seventeenth and eighteenth centuries as the European powers – the Portuguese, the French, the Dutch and the British hungrily eyed the riches that India had to offer. Britain won out and was left in control of India when the other powers moved on. Governing the subcontinent through the East India Company, huge wealth was won, often from the blood, sweat and tears of the indigenous people, and, more often than not, at a cost to their own prosperity and freedom.

As Indians grew restless at the end of the nineteenth and into the twentieth century, the long struggle for self-determination began and featured such great men as Mohandas K Gandhi, Jawaharlal Nehru and Muhammad Ali Jinnah. Eventually, Great Britain, exhausted and broken by the Second World War, divested itself of the 'jewel in the crown' of its empire and India was free.

The twenty-first century has seen a huge amount of growth

in the Indian economy but its challenges are many – illiteracy, disease, poverty, terrorism and corruption. But the future looks bright for this bustling nation of more than a billion people, but the story of how it arrived at this point is a fascinating one.

Chapter One

Ancient India

The Indus Valley Civilisation

India has been inhabited since at least the Middle Pleistocene era, between 500,000 and 200,000 years ago, and tools have been discovered, possibly dating back some two million years, made by proto-humans in the northwestern part of the Indian subcontinent. It was home to some of the oldest settlements in South Asia and a number of its earliest civilisations. During the Neolithic period – beginning around 10200 BC and ending between 4500 and 2000 BC – there was extensive settlement on the subcontinent following the end of the last Ice Age. Semi-permanent settlements showing the earliest traces of human life have been uncovered in the Bhimbetka rock shelters in the modern region of Madhya Pradesh. These date back to 7000 BC and herald the beginning of the South Asian Stone Age.

Prior to the discovery of early settlements at Mohenjo-daro and Harappa in the 1920s, it had been thought that the Vedic Indo-Aryans had created the earliest culture on the subcontinent and the third of the major civilisations – after Egypt and Mesopotamia – of early humankind. The twentieth century discovery, however, proved that the Indus Valley Civilisation preceded the Aryans.

As is the case today, India was subject to flooding and

it is likely to have been a flood that wiped out the first of the subcontinent's great civilisations. A series of floods of unknown origin are believed to have destroyed the work of agriculturalists who had been successfully growing cereals along the Indus. The key to their success was the management of the river's fluctuations, the seasonal rise of the river providing irrigation for their fields. They produced a surplus that had begun to stimulate trade and enabled a small-scale craft industry to prosper. Eventually, the settlements that had appeared developed into cities that vie with the contemporaneous societies of the Nile and the Euphrates for the title of 'the cradle of civilisation'. This civilisation was washed away sometime after 2000 BC by the waters and mud of the Indus. Indeed, it was forgotten until the twentieth century when Indian and British archaeologists discovered it while working at the ruins in Mohenjo-daro in Sind and Harappa in Punjab, Pakistan. They named it the 'Indus Valley Civilisation'. When it was later realised that this society stretched beyond the confines of the valley of the Indus, it was named the Harappan civilisation.

Much evidence of this people was brought to light, including tools, jewellery and artefacts that shed some light on their lives. It was learned that they traded by sea with Sumer in southern Mesopotamia. They also seem to have been able to write. Clay and stone tablets revealed symbols that were indicative of some kind of writing system that evolved into what is known as Indus Script. Sadly, however, the four hundred or so characters that were found have proved impossible to decipher. In fact, we know little of this society.

Harappa settlements have been found as far away from the Indus Valley as the Iranian frontier in Baluchistan and in the Pakistani province of Khyber Pakhtunkhwa. In India, sites have been uncovered in Gujarat, Rajasthan, the Punjab, Haryana, Uttar Pradesh and Jammu and Kashmir. Prevailing opinion does not hold that the Harappan culture was a uniform one with a central authority but its people's craft skills and their mastery of agriculture lingered on after the floods. Their skill at spinning and weaving cotton spread throughout the subcontinent until, by around 500 BC, it was practised everywhere. The Harappans may even have been the first people to use wheeled transport, although this achievement has been claimed on behalf of numerous others.

There are no grand structures at the Indus Valley sites, but supplying cities as big as Mohenjo-daro – which had around 30-50,000 inhabitants – would have taken a great deal of organisation and a sophisticated infrastructure. The largest structures at several of the sites appear to have been granaries in which surplus grain was stored. Trade was essential for survival and the further development of the culture. Bronze, tin and precious stones must have been imported as they cannot be found locally and it is clear that the peoples of Mesopotamia obtained commodities from the Harappans, including copper, gold, ivory and textiles. Harappan seals have been found in Sumerian sites, indicating documentation that might have accompanied shipped goods. The seals depict figures and symbols from this early civilisation. Tree deities have been recognised and a figure – sometimes known as Pashupati – seated in a cross-legged position that has been identified as bearing a resemblance to the Hindu god Shiva. It is sometimes called 'Proto-Shiva'. This figure has three heads, an erect phallus and is surrounded by animals.

The Harappans' demise left a void because, unlike other civilisations that went into decline, it was not replaced by another society. It simply vanished beneath the silt deposited by floods, leaving archaeologists with many questions but few answers.

The Aryans

During the second millennium BC, the semi-nomadic people that described itself in its literature as the *Arya* arrived in the northwestern plains, after sweeping through the mountain passes of Afghanistan. The Aryans left us the rich and important Sanskrit literary legacy, but there are questions as to whether they were, in fact, a distinct people. The Sanskrit epics are, of course, of vital importance to Hindus but, despite this, the *Arya* are a people that are not really revered. In fact, the term 'Aryan' appears nowhere in the literature and only emerged when Europeans began to study Sanskrit and its literature in the late eighteenth century.

In 1786, Sir William Jones (1746-1794), judge, philologist and founder of the Asiatic Society of Calcutta, discovered links between Sanskrit and Greek, Latin, German and the Celtic languages. This important discovery led to the philological study of what became known as the Indo-European family of languages. People began to believe that a shared ethnicity existed, that perhaps a single race had engendered all civilisation.

From a homeland somewhere on the steppes of southern Russia and Ukraine, the Aryans had spread to Iran, Syria, Greece, eastern Europe and northern India. Their highly warlike activities are recorded in the ancient Sanskrit texts, the Vedas.

Once it was thought that there was a gap of about 500 years, from the eighteenth to the thirteenth century BC, between the end of the Indus Valley Civilisation and the arrival of the Aryans. However, it is now believed that the interval between the two societies is not as clear-cut as that. Indeed, the Harappan way of life seems to have continued in some regions of South Asia right up to the Early Vedic period (*c.* 1500 BC) and there are traces – such as the keeping of horses – of early Indo-Aryan migrations into South Asia during the Late Harappan phase. This does not imply, however, that the early Indo-Aryans were direct ancestors of the later Rigvedic people. It seems that they were absorbed into the Indus civilisation and were probably responsible for the continuation of some elements of the Harappan civilisation such as the worship of animals and trees.

The first evidence of these people emerges from upper Mesopotamia and Anatolia where, around 1380 BC, a treaty was agreed between a king of the Mitanni who were based in northern Syria and southeast Anatolia and the Hittite ruler Suppiluliuma I (*r. c.* 1344-1322 BC). The treaty invoked Vedic gods. Sanskrit words have also been found in a horse-training manual excavated at the Hittite capital, Hattusa near the modern city of Bogazkale. However, this fact does not establish a direct connection between the Mitanni kingdom and the Vedic Aryans. It is more likely that at the same time as the Aryans were migrating from Central Asia to India – between about 2000 and 1400 BC – they were simultaneously migrating to West Asia.

The Vedic Aryans

The body of texts known as the Vedas is composed in Vedic Sanskrit and represents the oldest Sanskrit literature and the oldest Hindu scriptures. They are considered by Hindus to be *apauruseya*, which means that they were not composed by man but – to orthodox Indian theologians, at any rate – they are revelations experienced by ancient sages during periods of intense meditation. However, the great Indian epic, the *Mahabharata*, ascribes the authorship of the Vedas to the Hindu deity, Brahma.

There are four Vedas – the *Rigveda*, the *Yajurveda*, the *Samaveda* and the *Atharvaveda*. They were written between *c.*1500 BC and 500 to 400 BC and were transmitted orally during the Vedic period and probably until around 1000 AD. The *Rigveda* is the earliest and largest of these texts. It contains a collection of 1,028 Vedic Sanskrit hymns dedicated to Rigvedic deities and 10,600 verses, in 10 books. Composed by priests and poets, the age of the *Rigveda* is still a matter for debate. Some say it was compiled over a period of at least 500 years – between around 1400 BC and 900 BC – while others say it was written between 1450 BC and 1350 BC or even between 1700 BC and 1100 BC. *Rigveda* translates as the 'Veda of Adoration' and it mostly contains verses in praise of deities, especially Agni (god of fire) and Indra (leader of the gods).

The *Yajurveda* is made up of archaic prose mantras along with some verses taken from the *Rigveda*. The mantras were each made to accompany an action in a sacrifice. The *Samaveda* is the Veda of chants, the Sanskrit word 'saman' meaning a metrical hymn or song of praise. It consists of 1,549 stanzas that derive entirely from the *Rigveda*. It was designed to serve as a songbook for the priests who took part in religious ceremonies.

Atharvaveda translates as the 'Veda of the wise and the old'. Although compiled later than the *Rigveda*, the *Atharvaveda* seems to deal with a culture older than that of the *Rigveda*. It consists of 6,000 verses that make up 731 poems and a small prose section. About a seventh of its words derive from the *Rigveda*. The poems deal with the curative properties of herbs and waters as well as diseases and deities that cause them. It also discusses herbs and magic amulets that drive out disease. There are poems on the subject of sin and atonement, political and philosophical matters and a beautiful hymn to the goddess Prithvi, Mother Earth.

These texts reflect the development of Indo-Aryan culture from the time of their first migration into the northwest to their settlement of land in the Ganges valley and the creation of their first kingdoms. They are thought to give a reasonably reliable depiction of the life and history of the Vedic period, the *Rigveda*, in particular, proving a good source for information about the daily life of the Vedic Aryans. They were warlike, semi-nomadic pastoralists who engaged in cattle raids amongst themselves and against their enemies, known in the *Rigveda* and *Arthashastra*, a Sanskrit work on military strategy, as Dasa. They lived – when not on the move – in tribal settlements made up of several villages headed by a tribal chief. There were warriors known as *kshatriya* and priests known as *brahma*. Ordinary freemen were known as *vish*. Their success in battle against the indigenous population has been ascribed to the two-wheeled chariot they used but their conquest of the Indian plains was none the less a gradual one, slowed by the resistance of their opponents or perhaps by environmental conditions. Meanwhile, battles raged between the Vedic Aryan tribes. A battle is recorded near the River Hariyupiya close to the Afghan border and a couple of hymns in the *Rigveda* describe a 'Battle of Ten Kings', won by King Sudasa, leader of the Bharata tribe. Helped by Indra, he overcame enemies who tried to defeat him by destroying embankments that prevented flooding. Overall, plunder and pillage were common.

The Vedic Aryans extended their territorial possessions from the mountain passes of the northwest to the western area of the Ganga-Yamuna Doab, 'Ganga' being another name for the Ganges and the Yamuna being its second-largest tributary. For a period, the Saraswati River in the Punjab appears to have been the Vedic base and it was in such river-filled lands that they exchanged their nomadic lifestyle for a settled one, based on agriculture. Their battles were now fought over access to water or better land. With the jungles still being inaccessible at the time, the texts refer to 'the great struggle for water and sun' but the people now began to clear the forests and introduce irrigation schemes.

However, it would take the arrival of iron to control the forests effectively. It is mentioned in the *Rigveda*, in texts dating back to 1100 BC, and archaeologists agree that this was the date when the metal was first used in northwestern India. There is, as yet, little evidence of its actual use in clearing the forests, but it was certainly used by the Aryans in the manufacture of weapons. In the thousand years before the birth of Christ – the Late Vedic period – Aryan society developed, trade increased and crafts such as carpentry, potting and blacksmithing became established. Small principalities emerged and philosophical thought flourished. A class structure also emerged. We have already noted the separation into the societal segments of priests and soldiers. As the Aryans developed into farmers, they employed the local indigenous people to work for them. *Varna* – meaning colour – was what distinguished the locals from the Aryans and this soon began to mean 'caste', and was applied to the Aryans themselves. A late *Rigveda* hymn deals with these distinctions. It is of huge importance in the future stratification of Hindu society:

'When gods prepared the sacrifice with Purusha as their offering
Its oil was spring, the holy gift was autumn, summer was the wood
When they divided Purusha how many portions did they make?
What do they call his mouth, his arms? What do they call his thighs and feet?
The Brahman was his mouth, of both arms was the Rajanya [Kshatriya] made?
His thighs became the Vaishiya, from his feet the Shudra was produced.'

Thus was the place of the Brahmin priests secured at the pinnacle of society but the caste system would only take on its current importance at a much later date.

Even in the Early Vedic age, there were kings, some of whom were hereditary. They are to be found in Early Vedic texts but they were not allowed to act without consulting all the male members of the tribe or a council of eminent men. In fact, there were also tribes that were governed solely by such a council, without a king, an early example of a type of democracy, as has been noted by later historians. In the Late Vedic period, however, the king usually emerged not through a vote by tribespeople as before, but as a result of a power struggle amongst the nobles of the tribe.

The Late Vedic culture was rural and lacked any kind of planning or even fortifications. People generally lived in small settlements whose houses were of mud and wattle construction and there were no bricks. Blacksmiths and potters were at work by this time. Vessels have been found at various sites of the kind still in use today. Status and wealth were signified by cattle that provided milk, acted as beasts of burden and pulled the plough.

The *Mahabharata*

The 106,000 verses of the great epic, the *Mahabharata*, are traditionally said to have been written by the revered sage Vyasa who also features in the story as the grandfather of the two warring families. It provides information about the development of the Hindu religion between 400 BC and 200 BC and is viewed by Hindus as both a text about *dharma* (in Hinduism the rights, laws, conduct and correct way of living) and a history. It is a mélange of mythological and instructive material with, at its centre, the story of a power struggle between two groups of cousins – the Kauravas (sons of Dhritarashtra, a descendant of the mythical King Kuru) and the Pandavas who were the sons of Pandu, the great warrior king of Hastinapur.

This narrative takes up around 20 per cent of the entire work, and the remainder is devoted to a collection of myths and legends. The epic is set in a period when Vedic sacrifice was coming to an end and sectarian Hinduism was becoming more popular. More than anything, however, the *Mahabharata* is about *dharma* – the correct way to live.

Archaeological finds of Painted Grey Ware, a type of ceramic produced from around 800 BC to 400 BC, in the important places that crop up in the *Mahabharata* provide evidence that, rather than being entirely fictional, the events described in it may actually have taken place. Interestingly, the type of dice mentioned in the epic have also been found at some sites.

Chapter Two

Gangetic Culture and Great Empires

First Kingdoms

As Vedic culture spread eastwards, driven, it is assumed, by climate change, the first historical kingdoms began to form and cities grew. The formerly fertile Punjab and Doab became more arid while the Gangetic jungles receded, making them more accessible. Land was a source of conflict between tribes as they fought for the best grazing and agricultural territory. There may also have been a desire to move away from areas that were under the control of powerful kings.

Vedic people also migrated to the north, moving eastwards along the foothills of the Himalayas, but the most significant migration was undoubtedly the eastward one and the period from the late seventh to the late fifth century BC was one of the most crucial points in the development of Indian culture. In the central area of the Gangetic plains the first kingdoms were established, while in the north, cities and towns developed. In the late sixth century BC, the area of what is now Pakistan was annexed by the Persian Emperor Darius the Great (*r.* 522 BC-486 BC). The end of this crucial period in Indian history saw the emergence of the first real Indian historical personality – Gautama Buddha (*c.* 563 BC or *c.* 480 BC-*c.* 483 BC or *c.* 400 BC).

In the fifth century BC, 16 principalities were established from the many small tribal entities that had existed before. Of these the most important were Kamboja and Gandhara, located in Northern Pakistan; Kuru, Surasena and Panchala in the western Doab; Vatsa in the eastern Doab and, to the north, Koshala; Magadhawas situated south of the modern city of Patna in the state of Bihar. Further east was Anga and Avanti was in Central India while to the east of that lay Chetiya. These *mahajanapadas* (translated as 'great realms') all centred on the Ganga-Yamuna Doab and the area to the east of it.

It has been speculated that the *mahajanapadas* were confederations of several tribes, and this belief is supported by the fact that a number of them enjoyed two capitals. It is also thought that, although royal power probably prevailed in the immediate area of the ruler, outlying areas enjoyed a great deal of autonomy.

At the same time, urban centres began to develop, and six major cities emerged – Rajagriha in Magadha; Varanasi in Kasi; Kausambi in Vatsa; Sravasti and Koshala in Koshala; and Champa in Anga. Other Indian cities date back to this period. Previously, towns had not been fortified but these settlements were protected by moats and earthen ramparts. The ramparts would later be replaced with brick walls. Inside the walls, there were public buildings as well as dwellings and later, following the flowering of Buddhism, stupas and monasteries could be found. Coins have been discovered, indicating that the inhabitants of these settlements had begun to develop a financial system and trade must have been flourishing as standardised weights have also been uncovered.

the ancient east. The genius of Cyrus was in being able to govern numerous ethnic groups. He offered equal responsibilities and rights to everyone as long as they agreed to pay their taxes and remain peaceful. He cleverly refrained from interfering in the local affairs of his subject states in matters such as religion, customs and trade.

In 530 BC, he traversed the mountains of the Hindu Kush to conquer the tribes of Kamboja and Gandhara as well as the areas of modern Afghanistan and Pakistan. Ten years later, with Cyrus's successor Darius I (r. 522 BC-486 BC) on the throne, the Achaemenid Empire straddled much of the northwest of the Indian subcontinent. In 515 BC, Darius conquered all the lands around the Indus and was in control of the Indus Valley from Gandhara to the area of modern-day Karachi, a region that would remain under Persian control for two hundred years. History does not tell us much about the governance of the Persian conquests around the Indus but they were said by the great Greek historian Herodotus to return the largest amount of revenue to the imperial coffers.

Early States

In the late sixth and early fifth centuries BC, the states of the eastern Gangetic plains began to coalesce into four major entities. Several of the *mahajanapadas* seized control of others, resulting in the establishment of Koshala and the Vriji tribal confederation, which controlled the area north of the Ganges; Vatsa, which, from its capital Kausambi, controlled the area where the Ganges and the Yamuna rivers met; and Magadha, which controlled the modern area of Bihar, to the southeast of the Ganges.

The king of Magadha was Bimbisara (r. 542 BC-491 or 492

BC) of the Haryanka dynasty that lasted from the middle of the sixth century until 413 BC. A great friend and protector of the Buddha who lived most of his life in the kingdom, Bimbisara is known for cultural accomplishments, including the construction of his capital, Rajagriha (modern-day Rajgir). He is regarded as having laid the foundations for the later Maurya Empire and, under his rule, Magadha became the greatest power in India. He began the expansion of his kingdom with the conquest of Anga in today's West Bengal, a move that probably gave him control over lucrative trade routes and access to the east coast. Bimbisara was in all likelihood murdered by his son, Ajatashatru (*r. c.* 492-*c.* 460 BC) around 491 or 492 BC.

Ajatashatru continued his father's expansionist policy, conquering 36 neighbouring states and creating India's first empire. His immense kingdom stretched from the Bay of Bengal to the Nepal Himalayas. It had taken Magadha only two generations to attain such power but after Ajatashatru there was instability. The throne changed hands often and, on occasion, there were two distinct claimants. Things stabilised a little under the rule of Mahapadma Nanda (*r. c.* 345-329 BC), who was from a lowly caste. The Roman historian, Curtius, wrote:

'... his father was in fact a barber, scarcely staving off hunger by his daily earnings, but who, from his being not uncomely in person, had gained the affections of the queen, and was by her influence advanced to too near a place in the confidence of the reigning monarch. Afterwards, however, he treacherously murdered his sovereign, and then, under the pretence of acting as guardian to the royal children, usurped the supreme authority, and having put the young princes to death begot the present king.'

He waged war on the *kshatriyas* – in effect a war on the political order – and by 326 BC, the Nandas ruled a vast empire encapsulating the entire Ganga valley, Orissa and parts of central India. Nanda achieved this with the biggest army in India's history – 200,000 infantry, 20,000 cavalry, 2,000 4-horse chariots and anywhere between 3,000 and 6,000 war elephants. This was all maintained by the rigorous collection of revenues and by the stealing of booty during raids on neighbouring states. With his capital at Pataliputra, his empire was bigger than any previously seen on the subcontinent.

Mahapadma was succeeded by his eight sons, each of whom ruled briefly. The last of them was overthrown by Chandragupta Maurya (*r.* 321-297 BC).

Alexander the Great

In May 327 BC, the Macedonian Emperor Alexander the Great traversed the Hindu Kush Mountains of eastern Afghanistan, fresh from the conquest of the Achaemenid Empire of Persia. For a year, he fought into submission the various hill tribes of modern-day North Pakistan before crossing the Indus in February 326 BC. King Ambhi of Taxila, with a kingdom that stretched from the Indus to the Jhelum, submitted peacefully, supplying 5,000 troops for Alexander's campaign against his neighbour, King Porus (*c.* 340-315 BC), the Hindu king of the Pauravas. Porus prepared a huge army that included around 2,000 war elephants but Alexander defeated him with a surprise night attack across the flooded Hydaspes River. Impressed by Porus's courage, the Macedonian ruler reinstated him as king and formed an alliance with him.

Alexander's progress eastwards to face the Nanda Empire of Magadha and the Gangaridai Empire (in the modern-day

Bengal region) was hampered by monsoon rains. But his troops were also exhausted by eight years of constant campaigning. At the Hyphasis River (Beas River), they mutinied and refused to go any further. Despite a stirring speech by Alexander in which he invoked the memories of past conquests, they were not to be moved. Alexander turned south, therefore, along the Indus, battling with tribes he encountered en route before heading west. Three years after he had first set foot in India, Alexander returned to Susa in Persia. A year later, he died, aged 32.

The division of Alexander's empire, and the inevitable struggles for power after his death, brought an end to his dream of bringing India – or at least a part of it – into the Hellenistic empire and by 317 there were no more Greek outposts in the region. It had been but a brief few years of involvement but the knowledge gained about the subcontinent at this time was useful right up until medieval times. And the Hellenistic states that emerged much later in the northwest of India were important to the development of Indian art and science.

The Maurya Empire

Chandragupta Maurya, who overthrew the last of Mahapadma's sons, would become the first emperor to unify most of India under one government. His father was killed in a border dispute and Chandragupta was, according to legend, left with a goatherd who raised him as his son. He was then sold to herd cattle before being purchased by a Brahmin politician, Kautilya about whom little is known, but he is traditionally credited as the author of the *Arthashastra*, a Sanskrit treatise on statecraft, economics and military strategy. Kautilya took him to Taxila where he was educated in military tactics and the arts. His military career is said to have begun fighting Alexander along the Indus but how he managed to overthrow the Nanda emperor is not known. He was in power by 320 BC and in the following years he consolidated his power using an effective secret service.

In 305 BC Chandragupta faced an invasion by Seleucus I Nikator (*c.* 358 BC-281 BC), a former general in Alexander's army, who had crossed the Hindu Kush mountains to reclaim Alexander's heritage in India. Seleucus had established the Seleucid Empire in the Near East, incorporating most of the territory that Alexander had conquered. But Chandragupta defeated him in the Punjab, gaining all of Seleucus's territories east of Kabul as well as Baluchistan. His empire was now huge, covering much the same expanse of territory that would constitute the Mughal Empire some two millennia later.

As described by Seleucus's ambassador, Megasthenes (*c.* 350-*c.* 290 BC), Chandragupta's capital at Pataliputra was a striking construction, fortified with palisades and in the shape of a parallelogram about nine miles by a mile and a half. It had 570 towers and 64 gates and was around 21 miles in circumference, possibly the largest city in the ancient world. Society there was rigorously demarcated, although apparently not in any hierarchical order. The first estate consisted of the Brahmins, followed by the agriculturalists who were exempt from military service and paid rent to the king who was considered to own all land; 25 per cent of all their crops was also given to the state. Herdsmen made up another grouping. The traders were the fourth estate and the fifth consisted of the soldiers who were looked after by the state. Next were the ruler's inspectors and spies. Finally, there were the king's advisers and officials.

Not much is known about Chandragupta's reign after his defeat of Seleucus but, by approximately the middle of the third century BC, the empire stretched as far as modern-day Karnataka which indicates that either Chandragupta or his son

Bindusara (*r. c.* 297-273 BC) had conquered those southern regions at some point.

Ashoka 'the Great'

Chandragupta's grandson, Ashoka (*r. c.* 268-232 BC) was one of India's greatest emperors, ruling almost all the subcontinent, from the Hindu Kush mountains in Afghanistan to modern-day Bangladesh in the east. The start of his reign was particularly bloodthirsty. In 261 BC, he conquered Kalinga on the east coast, capturing 150,000 and killing 100,000 in battle. But after this campaign, he renounced violence and turned to Buddhism. Much is known about Ashoka from inscriptions on pillars and rocks and on one is recorded his great remorse after laying waste to Kalinga:

'His Majesty felt remorse on account of the conquest of Kalinga because, during the subjugation of a previously unconquered country, slaughter, death, and taking away captive of the people necessarily occur, whereas His Majesty feels profound sorrow and regret.'

His embrace of Buddhism led to a rapid growth in followers in his empire. He started missionary work and ordered everyone in his empire to stop eating meat and to behave decorously. He sent messages of goodwill to the neighbours of his empire and his officials toured the areas for which they were responsible, ensuring that the rules of proper conduct he had established were kept. These principles were inscribed on rocks strategically scattered throughout his territories. He also dispatched ambassadors to countries of the West, amongst which were Greece, Macedonia, Cyrene and Epirus. They also visited southern India and the area of modern-day Sri Lanka which was personally visited by Ashoka's son, Mahendra. Buddhism would later cross from southern India to Southeast Asia and it was transmitted to Central Asia from northwest India. From there, it travelled along the Silk Road to China around the first century AD.

It can be seen from his inscriptions that Ashoka ran a hugely centralised administration. Magadha, which he ruled directly, was its heart and four large provinces outside Maghada were ruled by *kaumara* or *aryaputra* – princes – who acted as viceroys or governors. These provinces were divided into districts that were governed by *mahamatras* who ensured that their district liaised effectively with the central government. The outer areas probably enjoyed a greater degree of autonomy, however.

The distribution of pillar and rock inscriptions is a good indicator of the extent of the Maurya Empire. There are a number in the main parts of the empire and on the frontiers but no inscriptions have yet been discovered in the interior. Thus, it can be deduced that large areas of modern-day Maharashtra, Andhra Pradesh, Kerala and Tamil Nadu did not form part of the empire. Control of trade routes was vital to the empire, especially the northern route from Pataliputra to Afghanistan. The route west from Pataliputra to the port of Bharukacha (modern-day Bharuch) was also of great importance.

Ashoka's achievement was the consolidation of his empire instead of its expansion which would have resulted in the addition of not much more territory but the loss of thousands of lives in bloody warfare. He adopted the right conduct as his guiding principle and it was transmitted throughout his empire by the rapidly growing Buddhist community. He ruled, however, not just through this ideology and the power of his large army but also because of the weakness of central and southern India.

Invaders from the North

The Greeks, or, in Sanskrit, *Yavanas*, were amongst a variety of invaders who began to arrive from the northwest. They came from a Greek colony established by the Achaemenids in Bactria – northern Afghanistan. During Ashoka's reign, it had been declared an independent kingdom by Euthydemus I (*r.* 230 BC-200 BC) and much of Afghanistan was added to it in the decades to come. As the Mauryan Empire began to disintegrate, the Bactrians began moving southwards.

All that is known about this people is derived from their coins which were minted and die-cast as opposed to the primitive punch-marked coins of the Mauryas. From them we can learn the names of their kings, the titles by which they wanted to be known and the Greek gods with whom they wished to be associated. We even know what they looked like from their portraits on the coins. In fact, the number of kings shown on these coins seems to historians to be more than was possible in the time span of 130 years. It has therefore been speculated that perhaps there was more than one king at any given time, or perhaps that there was more than one kingdom. But, as an intrinsic part of the corridor that carried trade from east to west and vice-versa, Bactria grew wealthy and was also an important source of bloodstock. For these reasons, it is thought that the Bactrians may have been engaged in trade with the Indians rather than invading them.

Demetrius II (175-170 BC or 140 BC) was probably the earliest of these 'Indo-Greeks' to arrive. He fought alongside a man who may have been his brother, Apollodotus (*r.* 180 BC-

160 BC or 174 BC-165 BC) and the general, Menander (r. 166 or 155-130 BC), who would later become king himself. There is some debate about whether, fighting together, these three conquered all of North India or whether they took some of the region and Menander took what was left when he became king a few decades later. Menander extended his rule to Swat to the north and perhaps to Kashmir and further east. He seems to have joined forces with the kings of Panchala and Mathura – both located in the Ganga-Yamuna Doab – and raided along the Ganges. They stormed Pataliputra, defeating the presumably Shunga ruler.

The Greek geographer and historian, Strabo (64/63 BC-c. 24 AD) wrote in his *Geography*:

'The Greeks who occasioned [Bactria's] revolt became so powerful by means of its fertility and the advantages of the country that they became the masters of Ariana and India. Their chiefs, particularly Menander if he really crossed the Hyphasis to the East and reached Isamus [i.e. Yamuna] conquered more nations than Alexander. The conquests were achieved partly by Menander, partly by Demetrius, son of Euthydemus, king of the Bactrians.'

It is unknown whether Pataliputra was held for long, but it is known that Pushyamitra Shunga (c. 185 BC-c. 149 BC) eventually ousted the Greeks. However, they also faced a revolt in Bactria in which Eucratides (r. 171-145 BC) seized power. He may have been a Bactrian official or, as some scholars suggest, a cousin of the Seleucid King Antiochus IV Epiphanes (r. 175 BC-164 BC). He killed Demetrius when he attempted to regain power and also defeated Apollodotus. Eventually, however, this Greek kingdom was overwhelmed by a Central Asian tribe, the

Shakas, between 141 BC and 128 BC although northwest India remained successfully under Indo-Greek hegemony for some time to come.

Following the death of King Menander, his kingdom was divided into a number of smaller entities that survived for some time. Greek rule of this part of India left little in the way of political legacy but there were cultural resonances. These can be seen, for instance, on the coins of the peoples who replaced the Bactrian Greeks in the first century BC. Greek gods are conflated with Indian deities, elephants are depicted and kings are shown on horseback.

The Shakas, the Yuezhi and the Kushana

A new wave of immigration brought new peoples to northwestern India but it is often unclear who they really were, when they arrived, for how long they reigned and even where their territories were. The reign of Maues in the Taxila region has been dated to any time between 94 BC and 22 AD. He may have been a Shaka (also Saka or Saca), a Scythian tribe, although some believe him to have been a Pallava, a people who were perhaps the same as the Parthians of northern Iran. The Shakas ruled a large territory that incorporated the northwest and bits of central India from Gandhara down to Mathura and Ujjain, stretching as far as the coast of Saurashtra. The Parthians succeeded the Shakas during the first century. Both peoples were from beyond the Hindu Kush where there had been a great deal of conflict. China had built the Great Wall in the third century BC in order to keep marauding tribes at bay. Consequently, these tribes had been diverted west before heading south. The Shakas had pushed out both the Bactrian Greeks and the Parthians from Iran and then the Kushana (Yuezhi in Chinese), from modern-day Xinjiang and Gansu, and began to supplant the Shaka, moving down into India in the second half of the first century AD. It is unknown whether this was an invasion or whether they were welcomed by the indigenous people. They could have been allies or mercenaries or they may simply have been refugees. This spelt the end of the Pallavans or Parthians but the Shakas or Scythians were more adept at assimilating themselves into Indian society and had a greater impact on the country. The Yuezhi, on the other hand – especially during the rule of Kanishka – went on to establish an Indian empire of sorts.

The first Kushana kingdom was established around the time of the birth of Christ by Kujala Kadphises (r. 30 AD-80 AD). He united his people, attacked the Parthians and took Kao-fu (modern-day Kabul) and Ki-pin (modern-day Kashmir). His successor, Vima Kadphises (r. 90-100 AD) expanded Kushan territory in modern-day Afghanistan, Pakistan and northwest India. Kadphises I seems to have been a Buddhist, but his son Kadphises II appears to have been a follower of the Hindu god Shiva as shown by coins minted during his rule. Kanishka, actually the son of Vima Kadphises, may have succeeded Kadphises II although it is also possible that unknown rulers followed him. The extent of Maharaja ('Great King') Kanishka's empire can only be surmised. It is believed to have stretched from the Oxus in the west to Varanasi in the east and from Kashmir in the north as far as the coast of Gujarat in the south. Both he and his predecessor seem to have shared the objective of controlling the lucrative trade routes between India and Rome, routes that bypassed the lands of the Parthians. Around 120 ships sailed annually from the Red Sea port of Myos Hormos bound for India, according to the Greek historian Strabo and it seems that the trade was far more beneficial to India than

Rome. Roman historian Pliny (23-79 AD) bemoaned this fact when he complained: 'There is no year in which India does not attract at least 50 million sesterces.' It was a matter of serious concern to Roman statesmen. There was also a moral element to the more conservative Romans' distaste for the trade. Pliny further complained:

> 'Our ladies glory in having pearls suspended from their fingers, or two or three of them dangling from their ears, delighted even with the rattling of the pearls as they knock against each other.'

In 63 AD, during the reign of the fifth Roman Emperor Nero (r. 54-68 AD), gold became the most popular form of exchange for trade between Rome and India and this undoubtedly helped to increase the prosperity of the Kushanas and would have contributed to their rise to power.

Kanishka was another of the great spiritual leaders, like Ashoka and Menander. A Buddhist, he left behind a monumental stupa at Peshawar reported to have been around 390 feet in height and 268 feet in diameter, one of the wonders of the age. He hosted a Buddhist council in Kashmir that contributed to the rise of Mahayana Buddhism and was also a patron of the arts, especially the Mathura school of art that reached its zenith during the rule of the Kushanas.

Although he was probably a Buddhist, the coins of his realm display gods of numerous religions – Hindu, Buddhist, Greek, Persian and even Sumerian-Elamite – demonstrating the extent of his huge empire and his skill at maintaining peace in his territories. He was succeeded by Huvishka (r. 140?-180 AD) who may have ruled with Vashishka, possibly his brother.

Around the time when the Kushanas were in power in

northern India, a branch of the Shakas who controlled the area between Saurashtra in Gujarat and Malwa in western central India emerged as a powerful entity. They were perhaps initially subservient to the Kushanas but they became a force with which to be reckoned when King Rudradaman I (r. 130-150 AD) was on the throne.

The last of the great Kushana emperors was Vasudeva (r. 191-232 AD). Significantly, he was the first Kushana king to have an Indian name, indicating the extent to which the Kushanas were being assimilated. This is also shown by coins they produced that featured Hindu gods. They seem to have been in power until the early third century when Ardashir I (r. 224–241), founder of the Sassanid dynasty, defeated them. Ardashir and his successor, Shahpur I (r. 240/42 – 270/72) conquered all of Bactria and the remainder of the Kushan Empire in Central Asia.

The Dark Period

There were 500 years between the decline of the Mauryan Empire and the rise of the next major Indian empire – the Gupta. This period is often known as a dark period of Indian history in which foreign dynasties tussled for control of the north. However, it was a time of development of economic and cultural relationships between the states of Eurasia, and India played a large role in this. Buddhism spread through international trade and interaction between the Indo-Greeks and the Kushanas and became strong in Central Asia. Meanwhile, the southern part of the subcontinent was establishing important links with the nations of the West and with Southeast Asia.

Indian society and culture were changing. Popular new cults developed around deities such as Shiva, Krishna and Vishnu-

Vasudeva. As Buddhism and orthodox Brahminism fought for supremacy in the royal courts and in urban areas, these new cults began to gain ground. These were vital for the development of Hinduism and were helped by the Kushana rulers' association with Hindu gods. It was said that after a ruler died, he would attain a complete identity with the respective deity. This deification of a ruler, already customary in the worlds of the Romans, the Greeks and the Iranians now became the norm in India. Again, it would be important for the development of the Hindu religion.

There were major advances in Indian art. Under the rule of the Shungas and those who followed them, a distinctive new Indian style had emerged. It was to be found in the relief sculpture of the Buddhist monuments at Sanchi and Bharhut. The Sarnath school of art developed out of the merger of the Gandhara school which had a Graeco-Roman style and the Mathura school with its more Indian style. It laid the foundations for classical Gupta art.

Other developments added to the richness of Indian culture at this time and were important for the future of Hindu society. The compilation of the *dharmashastra*, the Hindu law books – the most important of which was the second-or third-century Code of Manu – and a resurgence in the use of Sanskrit show that the dark period was not, in fact, so dark after all and presaged the classical age of the Guptas.

The Guptas: India's Classical Period

The Guptas were, in all likelihood, local princes based around Allahabad or Varanasi. The first of their number to make an impact on history was Chandragupta I (*r. c.* 320-*c.* 335 AD) who called himself *maharaja-adhiraja* (overlord of great kings).

He made a good marriage to a princess of the powerful Licchavi clan – Kumaradevi – that had controlled most of north Bihar for centuries.

The reign of Chandragupta's son Samudragupta (r. c. 335-c. 380 AD) was marked by expansion and conquest. He seized the lands of his immediate neighbours before launching campaigns in the east and the south during which countless kingdoms and chieftains were subdued and forced to pay tribute to him. He appears to have controlled, either directly or indirectly, much of the Indian subcontinent, from Nepal and the Punjab in the north down as far as the Pallava kingdom at Kanchipuram in the southeast. It was the beginning of the 'golden age' of Indian history.

The system that the Guptas introduced became the model for all India's medieval kingdoms. The heart of the empire was an area that was directly controlled by royal officials. Outside this area lived the border kings who had been subdued by Samudragupta. These rulers paid tribute to him and were obliged to attend the royal court, but they were not obliged to join the emperor's army in time of war. There were still some areas of the region, between the central area and the borderlands, which were inhabited by unruly tribes that had never been subdued. The task with these peoples was to prevent them from disturbing the peace and stability of the central region. Beyond all of these were the lands ruled by independent kings with whom the Gupta court enjoyed diplomatic relations. Of course, some regions under Gupta control themselves became powerful entities, such as Pundravardhana in Bengal and the city of Avanti (now Ujjain). This has led some historians to describe the Gupta state as multi-centred. Samudragupta aimed to be a universal ruler and an inscription at Allahabad says: 'He was a mortal only in celebrating the rites of the observances of mankind [but otherwise] a god (*deva*), dwelling on the earth.'

It was during the reign of Samudragupta's son, Chandragupta II (*r. c.* 380-*c.* 415 AD) that the Gupta Empire reached its apogee. This ruler employed the best tactics of his forebears to advance his ambitions. He used marital alliance and was aggressive in his territorial aspirations. Thus, by the start of the fourth century AD, the Gupta territory had expanded to cover most of the northern subcontinent.

In the latter part of the century, however, like Rome, India began to be subject to invasions by the Huns from Central Asia. Initially, Skanda Gupta (*r. c.* 455 AD-467 AD) kept them at bay but around 500 AD Gupta tributary states in the northwest and Rajasthan began to switch allegiance to the Huns. It marked the beginning of the end for the Guptas and the empire was all but over by 550 AD.

When Chandragupta was given one of Seleucus's daughters in marriage, the Greeks also sent an ambassador to the Indian court. From 306 AD until 298 BC this ambassador, Megasthenes kept an invaluable record of the Gupta Empire, published in his work, *Indica*. The people of the empire, he recorded, were divided into seven castes – philosophers, husbandmen, shepherds, artisans, soldiers, inspectors and the ruler's counsellors. The philosophers were the Brahmins and the inspectors, on the sixth level, were officials who guarded morals. Husbandmen did not have to fight in wars, their work providing food too vital for them to be taken away from it. Crops were dependent on the weather. Therefore, the Brahmins' weather forecasts were vital to the survival of the people.

Megasthenes reported that there was no slavery in India, women were chaste and men were courageous. There were no locks on the doors of houses and other buildings and Indians always told the truth. Lawsuits were rare and Indians worked hard. India, he said, was divided into 118 kingdoms some of which had control of other kingdoms and principalities. Village communities seemed to him to act almost as independent republics. He wrote of the Indian economy:

'Gold, silver, copper and iron are abundant on Indian soil. Besides tin other metals are used for making a number of tools, weapons, ornaments, and other articles.

India has very fertile plains, and irrigation is practised widely. The main crops include rice, millet, a crop called *bosporum*, other cereals, pulses and other food plants. There are two crop cycles per year, since rain falls in both summer and winter. At the time of summer solstice, rice, millet, *bosporum* and sesamum are sown. During winter, wheat is sown.

No famines have ever occurred in India because of the following reasons:

- The Indians are always assured of at least one of the two seasonal crops.
- There are a number of spontaneously growing fruits and edible roots available.
- The Indian warriors regard those engaged in agriculture and animal husbandry as sacred. Unlike the warriors in other countries, they do not ravage farms during war conquests. Moreover, the warring sides never destroy the enemy land with fire or cut down its trees.

Hinduism

Hinduism was developing all the time and, by the early years after the birth of Christ, it was a devotional religion whose

43

rituals took place in temples. It retained the sanctity of the earlier Vedic texts and the Brahmin priest remained sacrosanct, notwithstanding the fact that Hindu worship was becoming more devotional and worshippers were turning to the gods Shiva and Vishnu or to Devi (the Goddess).

In Vedic times Hindus had seen rituals performed by Brahmin priests as central to their worship and to their attempts to understand and control the universe but the *Upanishads* and the later unorthodox religions considered it the aim of every human being to attain *moksha* (*nirvana* in Buddhism) in order to escape from the cycle of reincarnation. Thus the devotional worship of a particular god (*bhakti*) developed. Alongside that came the temple as the place of worship and the very centre of religious life. Formerly, in Vedic ritual, worship had most often taken place in the open and without any images, now the image (*murti*) of a specific god believed to embody that being was established at the heart of the temple. The new gods that were subject to such worship were celebrated in a new collection of Hindu texts – the *Puranas*. These were tales of gods such as Shiva, Vishnu and Devi most likely composed between the third and tenth century AD. They consist of 18 *Maha Puranas* (Great Puranas) and 18 *Upa Puranas* (Minor Puranas) composed of 400,000 verses. They are considered *Smritis* – Hindu texts attributed to an author that are traditionally written down but constantly revised – and not as the authorless *Srutis* of Vedic literature that were transmitted verbally through generations and remained fixed in their content.

Older gods remained in the pantheon but it was Vishnu, Shiva or Devi upon whom the *Puranas* focused attention.

Caste, Varna *and* Jati

The Portuguese word *casta* was borrowed to create the term 'caste' to describe the Indian social system. Other terms were *varna* which means class, and *jati* which means birth group. As early as the *Rigveda*, the four *varnas* – Brahmin, *Kshatriya*, Vaishya and Shudra – were evident and very early on these had become associated with an occupation, usually hereditary – priest (Brahmin), warrior (*Kshatriya*), farmer or merchant (Vaishya) and servant (*Shudra*). By the early *Upanishads*, one's position was determined by karma or how one had conducted oneself in previous incarnations. On the other hand, *jatis* were determined by clan, family or tribe – in other words, by birth. Social contact between *jatis* was restricted although there could be economic activity between them. They were local or regional and people of a *jati* would be aware of their status measured against other *jatis* in their locale. *Varnas* were nationwide; *jatis* were not. In addition, *jatis* could be upwardly mobile and attain a new *varna* status by adopting customs defined by Sanskrit texts as those appropriate to a higher *varna*. These had then to be maintained through several generations. The converse was also true and *jatis* falling on hard times could fall down in *varna* status.

Thus, the caste system permitted frequent changes in social status, *jatis* losing caste or raising it as economic circumstances changed through several generations. Kings in ancient India often originated from non-*kshatriya* roots and, as a consequence, in the fourth century some *Puranic* texts attempted to allocate royal lineages to them.

Birth groups meant that *varna* status could be allocated to people who did not fit into the *varna* classifications. There were many new or non-Aryan groups and these could be assimilated into Indian society by thinking of each of them as a separate *jati* and using the group's economic status and political power to allocate an appropriate *varna* status. Thus, a wide variety of different non-Hindu ethnic groups were inculcated into the Hindu *varna* system.

Women in Ancient India

There is a passage in the Laws of Manu that gives the impression that women were completely under the control of men in Ancient India. It says:

'Day and night men should keep their women from acting independently; for attached as they are to sensual pleasures, men should keep them under their control. Her father guards her in her childhood, her husband guards her in her youth, and her sons guard her in her old age; a woman is not to act independently.'

But from other sources it becomes evident that women had greater freedom than this suggests. In the *Rigveda* we see unmarried young women and young men often in each other's company and women played a part in some ceremonies such as the Horse Sacrifice that was carried out to mark the elevation or inauguration of a member of the *kshatriya* or warrior caste. And in the *Upanishads*, two women – Maitreyi and Gargi – take part in philosophical discussions.

However, by the first few centuries AD women were becoming excluded, were forbidden to know about the Vedas and were being described as an inferior class. They could only attain *moksa* after being re-born in male form. In Buddhism and Jainism, however, they were still allowed to access religious scriptures and there were stories of young women visiting temples unaccompanied as well as sculptures showing young women watching processions from unenclosed balconies.

There is a dichotomy in the Hindu scriptures' view of women. In the Laws of Manu a wife is seen as the 'lamp' of her husband's home. A wife who provides her husband with children is described as a 'Lakshmi', the name of the goddess of good fortune. At the same time, women and their sexuality are often described as dangerous and even uncontrollable. But she should serve her husband as if he were 'a god', according to the scriptures. It did not even matter if he behaved badly towards her, as 'it is because a wife obeys her husband that she is exalted in heaven'.

High-caste widows were forbidden from re-marrying and sometimes a woman demonstrated her loyalty to her dead husband by becoming a *sati* (the one who is true) by being burned alive with her husband's corpse. This was not obligatory for Hindu women and was never that widely practised. It was believed that the *sati* was reunited with her husband in the afterlife and she was believed in the short time prior to throwing herself on her husband's funeral pyre to be possessed of magical powers, allowing her to curse or bless anyone she wanted.

Widows were said to have bad karma for surviving their husbands and had to lead an austere life as punishment. They had to shave their heads, wear white saris and could not wear jewellery. They had to survive on one vegetarian meal a day.

Harsha

A great deal more is known about life in the empire that followed the Guptas than about any other ancient Indian kingdom. The

Harsha Empire was described by one of the great Sanskrit writers, Banabhatta (sometimes Bana) in his biography of the Emperor Harsha (also known as Harshavardhana) (*r. c.* 606-*c.* 648 AD), entitled the *Harshacharita* ('The Deeds of Harsha'). The empire is also described in the Indian travel journal of the Chinese Buddhist monk, Xuanzang (*c.* 602-664).

After the fall of the Gupta Empire, northern India was split into a dozen or more feudatory states. Harsha had inherited a small state in the vicinity of Delhi at the age of 16 and over the next four decades created an empire that stretched along the Gangetic valley from the eastern Punjab to Bengal and Orissa. It was an unwieldy entity and the Buddhist Harsha spent his time constantly on the road with his troops, distributing alms to Buddhists and Brahmins, listening to his subjects' complaints about the way they were being governed by his officials and living in temporary shelters made of grass that were always destroyed when he left them.

Banabhatta, something of an adventurer, became a camp follower and wrote about Harsha, often in glowing terms, as was always the case with such works, but he also displayed subtle powers of observation and showed a compassion for the poor that was rare in ancient Indian literature. He described the chaos of the Harsha army striking camp and marching off to engage the enemy in battle:

'In front went the field-kitchens of the chief-vassals. Standard bearers led the ranks. As the troops left their small huts hundreds of their friends came out to meet them. The feet of the elephants trampled the hovels by the roadside and the people came out and threw clods at their keepers, who called on bystanders to witness their assaults. Poor families ran from their wrecked and ruined huts. Oxen, bearing the wealth of unfortunate merchants, fled from the hubbub. Clearing a path through the crowd with the glare of their torches, runners led the way for the elephants bearing the women of the harem. Horsemen shouted to the dogs running behind them. The veterans praised the tall Tangana horses, which trotted so smoothly and quickly that they made travelling a pleasure. Unhappy Southerners upbraided their fallen mules. The whole world was swallowed in dust.'

Ruling all of northern India, Harsha called himself by the title *cakravartin* (universal ruler) and employed the same methods as the Guptas for controlling his territories, giving lands to and gaining tribute and subordination from the rulers he defeated. He was a convert to Buddhism and his reign was a period of peace and prosperity, his court a centre of culture attended by scholars, artists and religious visitors from near and far.

Harsha died in 648, after a reign of more than forty years. His two sons were murdered by a chief minister in his court and, with no heirs to inherit the empire, it disintegrated rapidly into small states.

By the seventh century, the subcontinent was dominated by elites who were part of a Sanskrit-based, Indo-Aryan culture. Hinduism, based in temples, was becoming pre-eminent amongst religions and this was particularly true in the south. The tribes who had been making incursions into India for the preceding centuries had all now been just about assimilated into local and regional society and the state of permanent war and intrigue amongst India's political rulers was now at an end.

Harsha was the last Hindu king to control a vast North Indian empire and in future it would not be local or regional politics that would have a bearing on Indian rulers, but matters outside

India and often far away, such as the caliphate in Baghdad or even the Parliament of far-distant Great Britain.

India from the Seventh to the Thirteenth Century

India's history from 600 to 1200 is confusing. It consists of regional centres of power that emerged in the seventh century and remained until the thirteenth. Harsha's kingdom was no more soon after he died, but his capital Kanauj was prominent once again a century later with the emergence of the powerful leader Yashovarman (r. 725?-752?). He in turn was defeated by another great leader, Lalitaditya (r. 724-760), ruler of the Karkota Empire of Kashmir. Although his empire collapsed after his death, Lalitaditya's contribution to Indian history was his defeat of the Arabs who had captured Sind and parts of the Punjab after 711.

With Kanauj as the centre of northern India for several centuries, those who ruled in the east gained more prominence. From the late eighth century, to the early twelfth, the Pala dynasty ruled much of Bihar and Bengal and was pre-eminent in the north for a while. The Sena dynasty supplanted them in Bengal in the twelfth century, although the region remained largely independent as a sultanate until the arrival of the Mughals for whom it became a province.

In the eighth century, in the Western Deccan, after the demise of the Chalukyas of Badami, the Rashtrakutas of Malkhed emerged as the pre-eminent power. For a brief spell in the ninth century it was the centre of political power in the whole of India but by the tenth century the Chalukyas of Kalyani were the main force in the Deccan. A regional power was established in the twelfth and thirteenth centuries by the Yadava dynasty in the north of the Deccan. Invading

Muslim troops established the Bahmani Sultanate early in the fourteenth century. Also in the fourteenth century, Vijayanagar on the southern edge of the Deccan became the capital of the last great Hindu empire that incorporated much of southern India.

In the 'Far South', on the southeast coast, the Pallavas, Cholas and Pandyas wielded political power in the major river valleys. The Pallavas were predominant in the south from the sixth to the ninth century and when they went into decline, the ancient Cholas rose up again, ruling the south from their capital at Thanjavur. In the thirteenth century they were supplanted by the Pandyas of Madurai. They would reign supreme in the region for a brief period until they were attacked and defeated by the troops of the Delhi Sultanate.

The four centres above were the most important hubs of political power in India around this time, but other, smaller centres of power came and went. The Western Ganga dynasty ruled in the mountainous area of southern Karnataka from around 350 to the eleventh century. The Hoysala Empire became pre-eminent after them. The east coast from Bengal to Madras was often under the control of the Eastern Gangas and the Gajapatis. Thus, the sands of power shifted often between 600 and 1200, no one centre retaining power for long. Neither could rulers expand their power much beyond their own regions. The balance of power was maintained and each had pretty much the same military might as their rivals. This created political stability and the development of distinct regional cultures. However, there was also frequent conflict, often featuring more than two powers.

Chapter Three

The Coming of Islam

The Prophet Muhammad

Born in western Arabia, the Prophet Muhammad (*c.* 570-632) created one of the world's great religions. Around 20 per cent of the population of the world are now Muslims who regard Muhammad as the last of the messengers of God after Jesus Christ and Moses. Muslims view Muhammad as having completed the work of the two prophets who preceded him which, to their mind, makes Islam the ultimate faith. At the same time, however, it must be remembered that Muhammad was not divine; he was merely a messenger.

The Prophet was a clever political leader and, as a result, in Islam there is no such thing as the secular state. The holy book of Islam is the Koran, but Islamic law is to be found in the *Hadith* and Muslims try to follow the words and actions of the Prophet and his followers. These laws are known as the Sunnah. Together, the Koran and the Sunnah constitute Islamic Shariah law. This provides Muslims with a guide as to how they should live their lives. It is a system of social morality and that means that a breach of Shariah law is not merely a contravention of the law of a state, but an offence against God.

Muhammad's conversion occurred late, when he was forty years old, at a time when the Arabian Peninsula was little more than a small collection of autonomous tribal states. They were nomadic peoples whose worship was animist – they worshipped spirits that had associations with particular places or areas. It was a lawless place but it had one overriding benefit. Everyone spoke the same language, Arabic. This helped to unify the tribes of the Arabian Peninsula and by Muhammad's death in 632 AD at the age of sixty, Islam had conquered Arabia. Within a hundred years of his death, the Islamic Empire – the most powerful the Western world had ever known – controlled vast territories stretching from Spain in the west through the countries of the Middle East and as far as the Hindu Kush. It was halted there and it would be three centuries before Islam took control of India. There were numerous attempts in the meantime but they were repelled by the courage and military organisation of the Hindu kingdoms.

Muslim troops had first entered India in the eighth century by which time control of the Islamic Empire was in the hands of a caliph – an Arabic word meaning 'successor', 'steward' or 'deputy' – who was based in Baghdad from 750 to 1258. Islam had already experienced some internal strife and was now split into two opposing sects. The Sunnis were the more numerous of the two, basing their teaching on the *sharia*, Islamic law as understood by special theologians or scholars who were known as the *ulama*. The Shiites were a minority sect that followed the teachings of the twelve imams, spiritual descendants of the Prophet. The mystic tradition of Islam would begin in the eighth century and between the thirteenth and the fifteenth century, it would spread across north India.

Dar al-Islam

From the very beginning of Islam, there were Muslims on the Arab coast along the trade routes in places such as Sind, Gujarat, Bengal, Kerala and Ceylon, who had arrived in these areas with Arab merchants, missionaries and sufis, travelling from the Arabian Peninsula. There were a number of incursions by the Arabs. Caliph Umar (r. 634 AD-644 AD), for instance, gave permission for three Arab naval raids during his caliphate.

The first actual conflict between a ruler of an Indian kingdom and the Arabs took place in 643 when the Arabs took on and defeated Rutbil, king of Zabulistan in Sistan. Many other incursions took place following this but none was completely wholehearted. It was not that the Indian people were strangers to such invasions, especially in the northwest which, for centuries, had been subject to frequent raids by the marauding tribes of Central Asia.

By 711, the Arabs had conquered the region of Sind in the west. Meanwhile, in the northwest, independent Persian Muslims were in control of the land between Persia and the Oxus River – now known as the Amu Darya. Turkic tribes converted to Islam from Buddhism. From the 650s, Muslim Arab traders settled peacefully along the west coast of India and Arab traders opened trade routes that connected the subcontinent with the Mediterranean and, in the other direction, to Southeast Asia. Muslim merchants were given land and were assimilated as *jatis* (a distinct group of clans or tribes) into local society although, of course, they retained their own faith.

Mahmud of Ghazni

In the late tenth century, an astonishing empire arose from the Turkic slave-guards of the Samanid Empire. At its greatest extent, it comprised modern-day Afghanistan and large parts of Iran, Turkmenistan, Uzbekistan, Tajikistan, Kyrgyzstan, Kazakhstan and Pakistan. In 993, the one-time slave Sabuktigin (r. 977-997) took the throne, founding the Ghaznavid Empire and immediately expanding its borders by capturing former Samanid territories. In 998, following Sabuktigin's death, his son Mahmud (r. 998-1030) defeated his brother Ismail at the Battle of Ghazni and succeeded to the throne.

After recognition of his rule by the Abbasid caliphate, Mahmud pledged a jihad to raid India every year and he fought between sixteen and twenty campaigns on the subcontinent, the first in 1001, a defeat of the Raja Jayapala (r. 964-1001) of the Kabul Shahis at the Battle of Peshawar. A year later, he ended the Saffarid dynasty with victory at Sistan, dethroning Khalaf ibn Ahmad (r. 963-1002). He then targeted Hindustan to the southeast, especially the fertile plains of the Punjab. Raja Jayapala's son, Anandapala (r. 1001-1010), tried to extract revenge, gathering together a powerful Indian confederacy but he was defeated and Mahmud took control of the Shahi territories. The elephant-based armies of the northwest were powerless before his elite mounted archers. He wrote to the caliph at Baghdad that he had killed 50,000 infidels and the same number of Muslim heretics and was granted the honour of being named as a fighter in the cause of Islam. Invasions of modern-day Afghanistan and Pakistan followed.

In 1014, Mahmud launched an incursion into Thanesar on the banks of the Saraswati Ghaggar River in the modern state of Haryana in northern India. After failing to take Kashmir in 1015, three years later he defeated a coalition of rulers in Mathura and, in 1021, was victorious over the Central Indian Rajput dynasty of Chandela Ganda. He annexed Lahore in present-day Pakistan in the same year. In 1023, Gwalior became a vassal state, and from 1024 to 1025 he raided and plundered Gujarat. The Indian kingdoms he captured were left as vassals in the hands of Hindu, Jain and Buddhist kings and wherever he went, he enlisted local people into his army. He destroyed and plundered a number of major Hindu temples, including those at Mathura, Kanauj and Somnath, returning to Ghazni with wagonloads of riches and thousands of slaves. He also kidnapped Muslim scholars and brought them to Ghazni where he established a wonderful library filled with books plundered from Persian libraries. A spectacular mosque was also constructed there.

Towards the end of Mahmud's life, he had to deal with an influx of Oghuz and Seljuk Turks from Central Asia. Initially repelled by him, the Seljuks eventually took the cities of Merv and Nishapur in 1029. In 1037, with Mahmud dead, they sacked Ghazni itself and, in 1040, defeated Mahmud's son Mas'ud I (r. 1030-40) at the Battle of Dandanaqan.

Chapter Four

The Delhi Sultanate

The Slave Kings

After Mahmud's death in 1030, the Punjab remained under the control of his successors for 150 years, an Afghan Muslim province in India, but Ghazni was itself about to lose its position of pre-eminence. In 1186, the Ghurids, a dynasty of Eastern Iranian descent, overthrew the Ghaznavid Empire when Sultan Mu'izz ad-Din Muhammad of Ghor (r. 1173-1202) captured the last Ghaznavid capital, Lahore. Unlike Mahmud, who had captured many lands but had made little effort afterwards to control them, the Ghurids showed great ambition.

In 1191 Muhammad was defeated on his way to Delhi by the Hindus at Thanesar in the Punjab. Re-grouping at Lahore, he marched into Hindustan two years later. Unfortunately, the Rajputs were engaged in family feuds at the time and were unable to unite to oppose him. He occupied Delhi and marched on to Ajmere. In 1194, he overthrew the Hindu ruler of Kanauj and also defeated Asni and Varanasi. The southern limits of Muhammad of Ghor's advance were Benares and Gwalior, although Behar was taken by his general, Bakhtiyar Khilji (?-1206) who also took much of Lower Bengal in 1203.

Muhammad of Ghor was assassinated while offering his evening prayers on 15 March 1206. He had put his generals in charge of the provinces of the north of India and after his death they established themselves as kings of those territories. In Delhi, the former slave Qutb-ud-din Aibak (r. 1206-10), whom Muhammad had appointed as viceroy, immediately declared himself to be king of all of India and his dynasty lasted from 1206 until 1290. Several of those who succeeded him were also slaves and it is for that reason that his dynasty has been dubbed the Slave Dynasty.

The Slave Dynasty faced a number of challenges. Firstly, it had to establish control over those Muslim generals who had seized control of provinces on Muhammad's death. Furthermore, they had to quell revolts by disgruntled Hindus. As if those were not bad enough, they also had to contend with invasions by Mughals from Central Asia.

By the death of Shams-ud-din Iltutmish (r. 1211-36) the third and probably the greatest of the Sultans of the Slave Dynasty, it ruled the whole of India north of the Vindhya Range. This took in the Punjab, the Northwestern Provinces, Oudh, Behar, Lower Bengal, Ajmere, Malwa and Sind. During Iltutmish's reign, India was recognised as a separate Muslim kingdom by the caliph in Baghdad. He was succeeded by his son Rukn-ud-din Firuz who ruled for a little more than six months, and he in turn was succeeded by the only female occupant of the throne of Delhi – Razia Sultana (r. 1236-40).

Mughal incursions and revolts by Hindus soon began to undermine the rule of the Delhi Sultanate. In 1245, Mughals made it into Eastern Bengal and for the next 43 years they raided repeatedly in the Punjab. Meanwhile, Indian clans such as the Ghakkars and troops of Mewat plundered the Punjabi Muslim provinces and almost reached the Delhi city gates. The Hindus of Malwa, Rajputana, Bundelkhand and along the Ganges and Jumna rivers as far as Delhi engaged in frequent revolt.

By the time the last Slave king, Ghiyas-ud-din Balban (r. 1266-87), was in power, the Delhi Sultanate was under attack from the Mughals, the Indian tribes, the Rajput clans and even the ruler's own viceroys. He was ruthless towards Hindu rebels, almost completely wiping out the Rajputs of Mewat which lay to the south of Delhi, executing 100,000 of them. However, the Slave Dynasty ended with the murder of his grandson and successor in 1290.

The Khilji Dynasty

In 1290, Jalaluddin Firuz Khilji (r. 1290-96) was the first of a line that lasted for 30 years. The Khilji clan had its origins in Afghanistan and once in power began to extend the Delhi Sultanate into southern India. Jalaluddin's nephew Alauddin (r. 1296-1316) led a small army of only 8,000 men into the Deccan, pretending to be a refugee from his uncle's court. This allowed him to launch a surprise attack on the city of Deogiri (modern-day Daulatabad) which was the capital of the Hindu kingdom of Maharashtra. Having plundered the city, he returned to his base on the banks of the Ganges and invited his uncle to come and share in the spoils of his raid. When the old Sultan arrived, Alauddin murdered him as he shook his hand in welcome. During the 20 years of his reign, he consolidated Muslim power in southern India after subduing the Hindus of the north by taking Gujarat in 1297; seizing Rintimbur from the Jaipur Rajputs three years later; capturing the fort of Chitor; and in 1303, defeating the Sisodia Rajput clan who ruled Mewar. Meanwhile, he saw off five incursions from Central Asia between 1295 and 1305.

The throne passed to a low-caste Hindu general, Khusru Khan (r. 1320) who had murdered Alauddin's son to bring the

Khilji dynasty to an end in 1320. While outwardly portraying himself as a Muslim, Khusru desecrated the Koran and mosques, placing Hindu idols in the pulpits. His reign was brief and he was captured by disgusted troops led by the governor of Dipalpur, Ghiyath al-Din Tughluq, also known as Ghazi Malik ('Fighter for Islam') (r. 1320-1325) who beheaded him. Thus began the Turkic Tughluq dynasty that would last for 93 years.

The Tughluq, Sayyid and Lodi Dynasties

Ghiyath al-Din moved the capital from Delhi and established it at a place four miles to the east, naming it Tughlaqabad. He was succeeded by his son, Muhammad bin Tughluq (r. 1324-51). Although he was something of a scholar, Muhammad had a terrible temper and he was merciless towards his enemies. He squandered his father's carefully accumulated riches on buying off the Mughal hordes, who frequently swept down through Afghanistan into the Punjab, and assembled an army for an invasion of Persia that fell apart because the troops were not paid and plundered Muhammad's own territories. He is also said to have sent out a 100,000 strong expedition against Yuan Dynasty China that was wiped out by bad weather in the Himalayas. In 1327, he issued an order shifting his capital from Delhi 800 miles south to Deogiri (in modern-day Maharashtra) and changed its name to Daulatabad, hoping that this move would enable him to establish control over the fertile land of the Deccan plateau. He also hoped that he would remove the threat of Mughal invasions which were centred on the Delhi region and North India. Daulatabad was well situated to enable him to govern both the north and the south of his territory. His subjects migrated, unhappily, and many died on the road south but in 1335, fearful that the northern borders of the sultanate were exposed to attacks, he shifted the capital back to Delhi.

Muhammad was distrustful of Hindu princes and officers and even lacked trust in his own kinsmen. All the important posts in his government were filled, therefore, with foreign Muslim adventurers who had little interest in the stability of the state. Thus, he had to contend with around 22 rebellions as parts of his empire struggled to break free of his control. Around 1340, the Muslim viceroys of Malwa, the Punjab, Lower Bengal and the Coromandel Coast all revolted against his leadership and the Hindu kingdoms of Karnata and Telingana won independence in 1344. Muslim governors in the Deccan also revolted and there was a mutiny in Gujarat. Muhammad's reign also brought an economic crisis because, following his many expensive campaigns, his treasury was empty. Therefore, he ordered the minting of coins made from base metal that would have the value of silver coins. This led to ordinary people minting their own coins and the economy collapsed, creating a ten-year famine that devastated the countryside.

Muhammad died in 1351, fighting rebels in the lower valley of the Indus, but he had lived long enough to witness the collapse of his empire. He had been a cruel and vengeful man who was also capable of good acts, as described by the Moroccan traveller and scholar, Ibn Battuta (1304-68 or 69):

'This king is of all men the one who loves to dispense gifts and to shed blood. His gateway is never free from a beggar whom he has relieved and a corpse which he has slain.'

Muhammad's nephew Firuz Shah Tughluq (r. 1351-88) came to the throne and remained in power for 37 years although day-to-day government of the Sultanate was for many years given to the very able Hindu prime minister, Malik Maqbul (?-1369) who had worked in the government of Muhammad. Firuz Shah became a popular monarch, possibly because of his mixture of Muslim and Hindu antecedents, and his reign was peaceful and prosperous. He wisely recognised some of the breakaway states and instigated schemes of public works, building dams, mosques and colleges.

The Tughluq dynasty did not have long to go, however, and soon disappeared in a welter of Muslim mutinies and Hindu revolts. It fell victim to the Mughal invasion of 1398 when the Turco-Mongol military genius, Timur (r. 1370-1405), who is historically known as Tamerlane ('Timur the Lame'), rode through the Afghan passes, leading a large force of Tatar troops. He launched an attack on the Delhi Sultanate, at that time ruled by Nasiruddin Mahmud Shah Tughluq (r. 1394-1412), and won with ease. The Sultan fled and Delhi was sacked and razed to the ground. For five days, Timur's troops massacred the people of the city. It would take a century for Delhi to recover.

On the last day of 1398, Timur's army was on the march again, crossing the Ganges and massacring the inhabitants of Meerut. He travelled as far as Hardwar before heading west back to Central Asia. With Timur gone, Sultan Mahmud returned to Delhi, remaining in power for another 14 years at the end of which the Tughluq line came to an end.

The Sayyids ruled in Delhi from 1414 until 1451 and the Afghan Lodi dynasty from 1451 to 1526. There were four Sayyid rulers and three from the Lodi and some of them ruled over little more than the city of Delhi and a few miles around it, the Hindu princes and Muslim kings of the rest of India being more or less independent throughout this period. The House of Lodi ended when the Mughal Babur (r. 1526-30) was asked by the governor of Punjab to attack the Delhi Sultanate. The last Lodi Sultan Ibrahim (r. 1517-1526) was defeated and killed at the Battle of Panipat in 1526 and was replaced by the Mughals.

Kingdoms South of the Vindhya Range

Three ancient kingdoms – Chera, Chola and Pandya – were located in the Dravidian country of southern India where Tamil was the language. The largest was Pandya with its capital at Madura. It was founded in the fourth century BC. The Chola kingdom's main centres were at Kombakonam and Tanjore, while the capital of the Chera kingdom from 288 until 900 AD was to be found at Talakadu in Mysore, a city now buried in the sand of the Kaveri River. The 116th king of the Pandya dynasty was overthrown by the Muslim general Malik Kafur in 1304 but the Muslims failed to consolidate their power in the far south and the Pandya kingdom continued to be ruled from Madura by a succession of Hindu dynasties until the eighteenth century. Its lineage has been found to stretch back some 2,000 years. The Chera kingdom, meanwhile, boasted 50 kings and the Chola 66. The Hindu kingdom of Vijayanagar lasted from 1118 to 1565, its capital located in the Madras district of Bellary and evident from the ruins of temples, fortifications and bridges.

In the early fourteenth century, the Muslim Bahmani kingdom of the Deccan emerged following Alauddin's conquest of the south. Zafar Khan, an Afghan general and governor appointed by Sultan Muhammad bin Tughluq, was victorious against the troops of the Delhi Sultanate, establishing the Bahmani kingdom with its capital at Ahsanabad (modern-day Gulbarga). He adopted the title Ala-ud-Din Bahman Shah (r. 1347-58) and his dynasty lasted for 178 years, until 1525. At its zenith, Bahmani kings ruled half of the Deccan, from the Tungabhadra River in the south to Orissa in the north and from Masulipatam on the east coast to Goa on the west coast. Although supported by the southern Hindu kingdoms of Vijayanagar and Warangal against the Delhi Sultanate, the Bahmani dynasty, in the main, represented Islam fighting against Hinduism south of the Vindhya Range. Even so its alliances led to a mingling of Hindu and Muslim and the Muslim troops were often led by Hindu converts. There was often trouble between the two Muslim sects, the Shiites and the Sunnis who made up the Bahmani armies, and the throne itself was occasionally imperilled by this. The Bahmani dynasty was at its most powerful in the first half of the fifteenth century, but by 1489 was beginning to break up.

The Deccan Sultanates

Following the demise of the Bahmani kingdom, five separate independent kingdoms emerged in the Deccan. They were five dynasties of a variety of ethnic origins that ruled the late medieval kingdoms of Bijapur, Golkonda, Ahmadnagar, Bidar and Berar in southwestern India. Situated on the Deccan Plateau, between the Krishna River and the Vindhya Range, they seized the opportunity to become independent when the Bahmani Sultanate began to weaken and collapse. These small states were rivals to each other but formed an alliance in 1565 against the Vijayanagara Empire, defeating it at the Battle of Talikota, and thus contributing to its downfall.

The Adil Shahi dynasty, founded in 1489 by a son of Murad II (r. 1421-44), Sultan of the Ottoman Turks, ruled at Bijapur. It would last until 1686 when it was captured by the Mughal Emperor Aurangzeb (r. 1658-1707).

The Qutb Shahi dynasty had its capital at Golkonda. It was founded in 1512 by Sultan Quli Qutb-ul-Mulk, a former

Bahmani governor who declared independence from a weakened Bahmani state in 1538. It was annexed by Aurangzeb in 1687.

With its capital at Ahmadnagar, the Nizam Shahi dynasty was founded in 1490 by a Brahmin, Malik Ahmad Shah Bahri. It was annexed by the Mughal Emperor Shah Jahan (r. 1628-58) in 1636.

In Berar – capital Ellichpur – a Hindu from Vijayanagar, Fathullah Imad-ul-Mulk (r. 1490-1504) established the Imad Shahi dynasty in 1484. It was annexed by the kingdom of Ahmadnagar in 1572.

Finally, there was the Bidar Shahi dynasty, created in 1492 by a Turkic former slave from Georgia named Qasim Barid (r. 1489-1504). The small Bidar territory remained independent until 1619 when it was annexed by the Bijapur sultanate.

On the downfall of Vijayanagar, only a part of its territory was annexed by the Muslim kings of the south. The local Hindu chiefs – *nayaks* – managed to hold on to their possessions and from them are descended the *palegars* – territorial administrators and military governors – of the Madras Presidency and the Maharaja of Mysore. A member of the Vijayanagar royal family escaped to Chandragiri where he established a family line that gave Madras to the English in 1639.

Chapter Five

The Mughal Empire:
1526 to 1540 and 1555 to 1857

Arrival of the Mughals

The Mughal Empire was established and ruled by a Muslim dynasty of Chagatai Turco-Mongol origin from Central Asia. It would grow to be the second biggest in the Indian subcontinent's history, extending for four million square kilometres at its peak, taking in large parts of the Indian subcontinent and Afghanistan.

Its founding can be dated to Babur's defeat of Sultan Ibrahim Lodi at the First Battle of Panipat in 1526. Babur and his successors were Turco-Mongols of the Timurid dynasty, directly descended from both the great Genghis Khan (r. 1206-27), founder of the Mongol Empire, and Timur. Born in 1483, Babur had succeeded 11 years later to the tiny kingdom of Ferghana on the Jaxartes River (now called Sir-Daria). In 1497, he took Samarkand, Timur's capital and, driven out of the Oxus Valley by a rebellion, he captured Kabul in 1504. In 1519, he began a series of incursions into India and, during his campaign of 1526, he took Delhi. A year later he defeated the Rajputs of Chittor who ruled over Ajmere, Mewar and Malwa. He extended his power as far as Multan in the south of the Punjab and Behar in the eastern Ganges valley. By the time Babur died, his vast empire reached from the River

Oxus in Central Asia to the borders of the Gangetic delta in Lower Bengal.

The Mughals were of mixed race, and after the death of Babur incorporated Rajput blood through marriages that were arranged with Hindu princesses. Babur was succeeded by his son, Humayun (r. 1530-40) who was born in 1508. When he came to the throne, he had to hand Kabul and the western Punjab to his brother and rival for the throne, Kamran Mirza (1509-57). This left Humayun with India to rule but the Mughals were hated by the descendants of the early Afghan invaders and he was driven out of the subcontinent. The force that made him flee in 1540, after ten years of fighting, was led by the governor of Bengal, Sher Shah Suri (r. 1540-45), who was a Pashtun. The Pashtuns were an ethnic group native to Afghanistan and the northwest of modern-day Pakistan. Sher Shah proclaimed himself Emperor of Delhi but was killed in battle while attacking the fortress of Kalinjar. His son Islam Shah (r. 1545-54) succeeded him but Humayun had now recovered Kabul and he returned to defeat Sher Shah's nephew, Sikander Shah (?-1559) in 1555. After briefly reigning again, he soon died.

Akbar the Great

It was with the third Mughal emperor, Akbar (r. 1556-1605), known as Akbar 'the Great', that the Mughal Empire really came into its own. The son of Humayun, he came to the throne aged 14 and his reign began, therefore, with a regent, Bairam Khan (?-1561) in place. Khan, a Turkoman by birth, had worked for Humayun and was, in effect, in command of the army that restored him to the throne. Under the title, Khan Baba ('the king's father'), he helped the young ruler to expand

and consolidate his territory in India, turning his small kingdom into a large empire. It grew to incorporate almost the entirety of the Indian subcontinent north of the Godvari River. However, his domination reached across the whole country because of Mughal military, political, economic and cultural power. Akbar's approach towards those he conquered was conciliatory. He used marriage and diplomacy to bring territories peacefully under his control and established a centralised administration so that he was aware of and in control of what was happening in the farthest-flung corners of his empire. He was ruling a culturally diverse empire but he employed policies that did not interfere with tribal ties and did not force Islam on his subjects.

Akbar began by advancing from the Punjab and re-capturing Delhi which Sikander Shah's general, Hemu (r. 1556), had taken. Panipat, where Babur had won thirty years previously, was again the battlefield and on 5 November 1556, the youthful Akbar, with Khan Baba's support, defeated Hemu. Thus, India finally passed from the Afghans to the Mughals.

When Akbar ascended the throne, India was divided into tiny Hindu and Muslim kingdoms. By the time of his death in 1605, he ruled an empire that was almost totally united and that was unfailingly loyal to him. The Muslim states that had resulted from the earlier invasions by various peoples including the Turks, Afghans and Mughals were fashioned into provinces and many of the Rajput nations and Hindu kings maintained their independence although he ensured that they were dependent upon his authority. Of course, there was always a military threat to fall back on but Akbar gave all his subjects political equality in his Persianised empire. All the sacred books and epic poetry written in Sanskrit were translated into Persian and, as well as demonstrating respect for Hindu laws, he showed an interest in the Hindu religion rather than proscribing it. He forbade some practices, such as animal sacrifice, trial by ordeal and child marriage, however. He permitted Hindu widows to re-marry and although he did not ban the practice of *sati* he ensured that widows could not be forced to participate in the ritual.

With Hindu support, Akbar subdued the Muslim kingdoms of north India and defeated Hindu powers from the Punjab to Bahar. Lower Bengal was seized from the Afghan descendants of Sher Shah and for almost two centuries it would remain a part of the Mughal Empire, governed by officials appointed in Delhi. Only in 1765 did it leave the empire, as an imperial grant to the British. Meanwhile, Orissa was taken by Akbar's Hindu general, Todar Mal (?-1589), in 1575. Gujarat was taken by 1573 and Malwa had fallen to the empire the year before. Kashmir was captured in 1587 but continued to rebel until 1592; Sind was annexed in 1592; and Kandahar in 1594. The empire of Akbar was now vast, stretching from Afghanistan, across India north of the Vindhya Range, over to Orissa in the east and Sind in the west. He made Agra his new capital, calling it Akbarabad. It would remain capital until Shah Jahan made Shahjahanabad (Old Delhi) his base in 1649.

It proved more difficult to consolidate the Mughal Empire in the south. For the twelve years after 1586, Akbar was up against the courage and wiliness of Chand Bibi (1550-1599) the Muslim warrior queen of Ahmadnagar. She succeeded in uniting the Abyssinian and Persian factions in southern India and made alliances with other Muslim states. Akbar attacked in 1599 and she put up a brave defence, but she was assassinated by mutinous troops who believed a false rumour that she was in cahoots with the Mughals. Akbar also took Khandesh but returned to his capital in 1601, perhaps believing that the conquest of the south was beyond even his capabilities.

He left behind a well-organised empire, separated into provinces, each of which had a governor who was in charge of both civil and military matters. He had also made efforts to prevent his troops from mutinying and rebelling, paying his generals with cash instead of grants of land, as had previously been the practice. He also prevented his generals in the provinces from seeking independence by creating an almost feudal set-up, Hindu tributary princes being equal to the Mughal nobles.

Akbar's Successors

Akbar's son, Salim, took the throne under the imperial name of Jahangir (r. 1605-1627) which means 'conqueror of the world'. He ruled for 22 years but for much of that time he was quelling rebellions by his sons, dealing with his wife Nur Jahan (1577-1645) whose persistent plotting is said to have troubled him in his final years on the throne, and simply enjoying himself. He failed to extend the territories of the empire he had inherited from his father, despite wars in southern India and the Deccan. By the close of his life, his own son, Prince Khurram had fled to the Deccan where he joined in alliance with the Abyssinian prime minister of the Ahmadnagar Sultanate, Malik Ambar (1549-1626). Ambar had managed, against the odds, to maintain the independence of Ahmadnagar. Meanwhile, the Rajputs were starting to stir, hoping to regain their independence.

Jahangir's wife Nur Jahan, although described as 'the light of the world', actually cast a huge shadow across his reign. A strong, charismatic woman, she wielded an inordinate amount of influence over her husband and is considered by many historians to have been the real power behind the throne. She was in charge of the imperial seal, implying that before anything was given legal validity, it had first to be seen and approved by her.

She had been born into an impoverished noble family and she and Jahangir had fallen in love while still young. Emperor Akbar, however, was against the relationship and married her off to a soldier. When he took the throne, Jahangir ordered that she be divorced from her soldier husband. The husband refused to comply and Jahangir had him murdered. She moved to the royal palace where she began to exert influence over the emperor. At first all was well, but soon the resentment and jealousy felt against her by the imperial princes and Jahangir's generals began to manifest itself.

After Jahangir's death, his son Prince Khurram became emperor as Shah Jahan (r. 1628-58). He immediately dealt with Empress Nur Jahan, banishing her from the palace, and murdered his brother, along with every other member of his family who might have sought to usurp his throne. He proved to be a just ruler and ably managed the finances of the empire. Kandahar was finally lost but the empire's borders were extended in the Deccan and in the south. Ahmadnagar was at last annexed by the empire in 1636 and Bidar fort was captured in 1657. Bijapur and Golkonda became tributary states and would eventually succumb following the accession of Shah Jahan's successor, Aurangzeb (r. 1658-1707).

During his reign great structures were built that are amongst some of the most magnificent monuments to the Mughal Empire. He had the splendid mausoleum of the Taj Mahal constructed at Agra, a memorial to his favourite wife Mumtaz Mahal (1593-1631). He also supervised the construction of the beautiful marble Moti Masjid ('Pearl Mosque') inside the Agra fort that had been re-built in red sandstone by Akbar. He transferred the seat of government back to Delhi, adorning the city with many wonderful buildings, such as the great mosque, the Jama Masjid which was built between 1644 and 1656 and reputedly cost a million rupees. The Palace of Delhi was constructed in marble and stone in the form of a giant parallelogram 1,600 by 3,200 feet.

Aurangzeb

Abu'l Muzaffar Muhi-ud-Din Muhammad Aurangzeb Alamgir, commonly known as Aurangzeb, was the third son of Shah Jahan and Mumtaz Mahal. Under him, the Mughal Empire reached its greatest extent. But before acceding to the imperial throne, he was rivalled by his brother Dara Shikoh (1615-59) designated as next emperor by Shah Jahan.

When Shah Jahan became ill in 1657, a war of succession seemed inevitable. Although the emperor's health recovered on this occasion, it was too late for either of the brothers to withdraw and hostilities broke out between them. Aurangzeb displayed great military skill, guile and a ruthless determination to win, defeating Dara in the Battle of Samurgah in May 1658 and proclaiming himself emperor. He had a number of his family murdered and imprisoned his father in his palace in Agra until his death eight years later in 1666.

His reign can be split in two. The first years until 1680 proved him to be a capable ruler, a Muslim leading an empire that was both Hindu and Muslim. He was hated for the ruthlessness he displayed but admired for his energy and skill. For much of this time, he was engaged in preventing the Persians and the Central Asian Turks from making progress in the northwest of the empire. He also had problems with the leader of the Marathas, Shivaji (r. 1674-80) who raided the Gujarati port of Surat twice, in 1664 and 1670. He followed the same method with the Maratha ruler as his great-grandfather Akbar had – he defeated him, and then gave him an imperial rank, allowing him to remain in position, but subject to the empire. Shivaji reneged on his side of the bargain, fleeing to the Deccan where he died in 1680, still ruling an independent kingdom.

It was around this time that Aurangzeb seems to have undergone a change of thinking. He became a pious Muslim and began to treat Hindus as subordinates rather than the equals they had previously been. He became increasingly puritanical as his reign progressed, and his edicts were enforced by officials called *muhtasibs* – censors of morals. He also decided to annex the Maratha kingdom, rather than just subdue it. In 1679, he re-instated the *jizya*, a poll tax on non-Muslims that Akbar had abolished during his reign. He also destroyed numerous temples, amongst which were three of the most sacred to Hindus – the Kashi Vishwanath temple, the Kesava Deo temple and the Somnath temple – replacing them with mosques. The Rajputs rebelled against him in 1680 and there was little enthusiasm for the Mughal Empire amongst Hindus.

He still enjoyed success, however. In 1686-87, his troops took the Deccan kingdoms of Bijapur and Golkonda but the insecurity and lack of stability in the empire led to an economic crisis. This was not helped by war with the Marathas who spread the conflict across southern India by employing guerrilla tactics. His focus on the south led to a vacuum in the north of the empire and the government of the region weakened. There was unrest amongst those living on the land resulting in the growth of religious movements such as the Satnamis and the Sikhs in the Punjab. The Satnamis were crushed by the emperor in 1672 and Aurangzeb executed the Sikh leader Tegh Bahadur three years later for refusing to embrace Islam. This led to conflict with the Sikhs for the remainder of his reign.

Aurangzeb ruled for almost half a century, extending the empire to the south as far as Tanjore (modern-day Thanjavur) and Trichinopoly (modern-day Tiruchirappali). But the cracks had begun to show. The militancy of the Sikhs and the Jats was a warning of trouble to come in the north of the empire and both Hindus and Rajputs had been angered by Aurangzeb's attitude towards them. He left a number of incipient problems that would lead, inevitably, to the collapse of the Mughal Empire in the middle of the eighteenth century.

End of Empire

After Aurangzeb, emperors tended to be pawns in the hands of powerful statesmen or generals. These wily operators placed the emperor on the throne, controlled him while he was there and, when it suited them, killed him and replaced him with another puppet. The decline of the empire had well and truly begun. As Vizir-e-Azam, or Prime Minister, the unscrupulous General Zulfiqar Khan (1657-1713) controlled two of the six emperors that followed Aurangzeb – Bahadur Shah (r. 1707-12) and Jahander Shah (r. 1712-13). Bahadur was the first Mughal emperor to rule over an empire that was crippled by unbridled revolts and Jahandar was an incompetent who ruled for just under a year before he was killed in battle at Agra. The victor in this battle was the next emperor, Farrukhsiyar (r. 1713-19) who won with the support of the powerful Mughal army generals, the Sayyid brothers, Syed Hassan Ali Khan Barha (1666-1722) and Syed Hussain Ali Khan Barha (1668-1720). The brothers became known as 'king-makers'.

By 1720, however, the break-up of the empire had begun. Chin Qulich Khan had been given the title Nizam-al-Mulk – the title for rulers of Hyderabad – in 1713 by Emperor Farrukhsiyar.

This title was used by rulers of Hyderabad until 1947. Emperor Muhammad Shah (r. 1719-48) added Asaf Jah to the title in 1725. In 1724, the Nizam declared himself independent ruler of the Deccan where he had been viceroy from 1720.

At Awadh (Oudh to the British), Saadat Ali Khan (r. 1722-39), who had risen to be prime minister of the empire, more or less created his own dynasty as the Nawab of Awadh. He was succeeded by his son-in-law, Safdar Jung (r. 1739-54) and he, in turn, was followed by his son Shuja-ud-Daula (r. 1753-75). The latter is best known for his important participation in two key battles in Indian history. The Third Battle of Panipat was fought in 1761 between the Maratha Empire and the invading forces of the King of Afghanistan, Ahmad Shah Durrani (r. 1747-72) who was supported by two Indian allies – the Rohilla Afghans of the Doab, and the army of Shuja-ud-Daula. This battle was the biggest of the eighteenth century, recording perhaps the largest number of casualties in a single day in a classic formation battle between two armies. Between 90,000 and 150,000 died. It halted the Maratha advance in the north and destabilised the Maratha Empire for perhaps a decade. It also overthrew the Mughal Emperor Shah Jahan III and restored the rightful emperor, Shah Alam II. Shuja-ud-Daula also participated in the 1764 Battle of Buxar between his own forces, allied with those of Mir Qasim, Nawab of Bengal, and the Mughal Emperor Shah Alam II, against troops of the British East India Company, led by Hector Munro, 8th Laird of Novar (1726-1805).

Meanwhile, the Mughal Empire's Hindu population was also seeking self-determination. Ajit Singh (r. 1699-1724) declared independence for Marwar and most of the Rajputs broke away from the empire in 1715. The Marathas were now on the scene, having subjugated much of the south. They obtained Malwa from the Mughals in 1749 and Orissa and Bengal in 1751.

External Enemies

In 1739, the Persian ruler, Nadir Shah (r. 1736-47), swept into India. A military genius, sometimes described as the 'Napoleon of Persia', Nadir Shah was a Turcoman who rose to power during a period of anarchy in Persia. Having succeeded in reuniting Persia and defeating invaders such as the Russians and the Ottomans, he overthrew the Safavids who had ruled Persia for two centuries and declared himself Shah. The empire he built incorporated Armenia, Azerbaijan, Georgia, the North Caucasus, Iraq, Turkey, Turkmenistan, Afghanistan, Tajikistan, Uzbekistan, Pakistan, North India, Oman and the Persian Gulf.

The Mughal Empire was ripe for the taking. The nobles were recalcitrant, provinces were declaring themselves independent and the Maratha Empire was advancing into Mughal territory from the southwest. Nadir Shah crossed the border and defeated the Mughal forces defending the Khyber Pass, even though outnumbered by two to one. He crossed the Indus before the end of 1738 and advanced on Delhi where Emperor Muhammad Shah began to assemble a 300,000-strong army. In February 1739, at the Battle of Karnal, Nadir Shah defeated the Mughals who outnumbered his army by six to one in just three hours. Delhi was sacked and 20,000 of its inhabitants were killed in one day. Muhammad Shah pleaded with the Persian ruler for mercy and, in return for the keys to the vast Mughal treasury, Nadir Shah agreed to withdraw. That is how the splendid Peacock Throne which had been commissioned by Shah Jahan in the early seventeenth century ended up in Persian hands, although it soon disappeared, never to be seen again except in the form of a replica made in India. Nadir Shah is said to have escaped over the passes of the Indian northwest carrying booty worth around the equivalent of $155 million.

The Persian attack was followed by six invasions between 1747 and 1767 from Afghanistan. They were led by Ahmad Shah Durrani (r. 1747-72), who, after the assassination of Nadir Shah in 1747, had been chosen as King of Afghanistan. After establishing the Durrani Empire with its capital at Kandahar, he and his troops pillaged the north, exhibiting ruthless cruelty as they went. In 1752, he gained the Punjab from the Mughals and five years later, he and his men subjected Delhi to untold cruelty while his troops pillaged through the countryside, killing, plundering and destroying Hindu temples and holy places. Whole regions and large cities were denuded of people who fled in fear. One account by the Tyrolean Jesuit missionary and geographer, Joseph Tieffenthaler (1710-85), graphically describes the actions of this bloodthirsty horde:

'They burned the houses together with their inmates, slaughtering others with the sword and the lance; hauling off into captivity maidens and youths, men and women. In the temples they slaughtered cows and smeared the images and pavement with the blood.' (Cows were, of course, sacred to Hindus.)

Between 1748 and 1761 as the British and the French fought in southern India, the Mughals lost Karnataka. The English Lord Clive (1725-74) obtained Orissa, Bengal and Bihar in 1765 from the titular Mughal emperor and the Mughal Empire now barely existed. The British moved in and used the Mughal Empire as a structure on which they could pin their ambition, installing puppet emperors whose power extended little further

than their palace walls. Beyond those walls, the battle was on
for the spoils, the Marathas, the British and the Sikhs fighting
for ultimate control of the subcontinent.

Chapter Six

The Maratha Empire: 1675 to 1818

Shivaji

The Maratha Empire's founder was an aristocrat of the Bhonsle clan, Chattrapati Shivaji (r. 1674-80). Born in 1627, Shivaji was at the forefront of a party formed by the Hindu tribes of the Deccan that was opposed to the imperial armies from the north as well as the Muslim kingdoms of the south. This meant that there were a number of competing elements in the Deccan – the troops of the Delhi Empire; the armies of Ahmadnagar and Bijapur, the remaining two independent Muslim states in the region; and the forces of the local Hindu tribes that would evolve into the Maratha confederacy.

While Shah Jahan and then Aurangzeb were in power and trying to conquer the southern Muslim kingdoms, this Hindu grouping sided sometimes with them and sometimes with the Muslim kingdoms. The latter were more than a match for the imperial army but when the Delhi Empire was supported by the Marathas, their combined force was too much for them. This, of course, put Shivaji in the driving seat and, basing himself in impregnable hill forts in the Western Ghats, he became the dominant power in southern India. Drawing his warriors from the vast territory of Maharashtra that stretched from the Behars in central India to an area close to the south of the Bombay Presidency, he had an inexhaustible supply of willing fighters. They were the peasant farmers of southern India and were available to him any time apart from when they were planting or at harvest. This meant that he did not have the great expense of a standing army and he was able to pay them from plunder won in his raids.

In 1664, Shivaji pronounced himself raja (king) and started coining money in his own name and the following year he was fighting on the side of the Mughals against the independent Muslim state of Bijapur. He visited Delhi in 1666 and had to flee after being arrested. He died in 1680.

It might have served the Mughal Empire better if Aurangzeb had made peace with the Indian Muslims and focused instead on the Marathas, turning the united force of Islam against the Hindus. And there was little doubt that the Hindu confederacy was growing into a force to be reckoned with. Instead, he followed his plan to annex southern India's Muslim kingdoms, leaving the Marathas to grow increasingly powerful.

The Maratha Confederacy

Shivaji's son Sambhaji (r. 1680-89) succeeded him, remaining on the throne until 1689, and spending much of that time engaged in wars with both the Mughals and the Portuguese who had established settlements on India's southwestern coast. In 1689, however, he was taken prisoner by Aurangzeb, cruelly tortured and beheaded. His six-year-old son and heir Shahuji (r. 1708-49) was kept prisoner until Aurangzeb's death. While the boy was imprisoned, Rajaram (r. 1689-1700), his half-brother, took the throne. The Mughals were, at the time of his accession, laying siege to Raigad and the new monarch had to flee to Vishalgad and then Gingee for safety. Under brilliant commanders such as Santaji Ghorpade (?-1696), Dhanaji Jadhav (1650-1708) and Parshuram Pant Pratinidhi (1660-1718), the Marathas began to attack Mughal territory, capturing numerous forts. When Rajaram offered Aurangzeb a truce in 1697, the Mughal leader rejected it.

Rajaram died in 1700 and was succeeded by his queen, Tarabai (1675-1761) who took the throne in the name of her son, Shivaji II (r. 1696-1726). By 1705, she had led the Marathas across the Narmada River and into Malwa which was, at the time, in Mughal hands.

In 1707, the new emperor, Bahadur Shah released Shahuji, although his mother remained in captivity in order to force him to stick to the conditions of his release. Shahuji challenged Tarabai and her son, claiming to be the rightful ruler. Finally accepted as leader of the Marathas, he appointed Balaji Vishwanath (1662-1720) as his Peshwa or Prime Minister. Holding office from 1712 to 1720, Balaji was the first of a series of hereditary Peshwas who came from the Hindu Chitpavan Brahmin family. As time passed, the Peshwa came to have more power than the Maratha monarch who became little more than a figurehead. After Balaji Vishwanath's death in 1720, his son Baji Rao (1700-40) took on his father's role, expanding the empire from 3 per cent to 30 per cent of modern India. He was followed as Peshwa by his son, Balaji Baji Rao (1720-61), known as Nana Saheb. It was during his tenure that the Maratha Empire was transformed into a confederacy in which individual chiefs were more powerful and that Maratha territory reached its zenith. By 1751, it stretched north into Rajasthan, Delhi and the Punjab and in the south it extended as far as Karnataka and the land of the Tamils. Adept at finance and organisation, Nana Saheb was not a soldier like his father and, by the end of his life, the role of the Peshwa was very different to what it had previously been. It may have been his lack of military prowess that led to his failure to recognise the seriousness of the Durrani incursions into northern India. This eventually led to the devastating defeat of the Marathas at the Third Battle of Panipat in 1761. This was a huge setback for Nana Saheb and he died a few months later, succeeded as Peshwa by his son Madhav Rao I (1774-95). He took over when the confederacy appeared to be in terminal decline, threatened by internal tensions as well as by exterior forces such as the Durranis.

In the south the Peshwa ruled supreme, but in the north there were four ruling branches of Marathas – the Sindhia, the Holkar, the Bhonslas of Nagpur and the Gaekwars of Baroda. After the disaster of Panipat, not much was heard of the Holkars and the Sindhia for a few years, but, by 1771, they had established themselves in Malwa and had invaded the provinces of Rajput, Jat and Rohilla. They allowed the Mughal emperor Shah Alam to remain on the throne following his defeat by Sir Hector Munro's British troops at Buxar in 1764, but he was their captive until they themselves lost to the British in the Second Maratha War (1803-05).

The Bhonslas of Berar and the Central Provinces operated from their base at Nagpur. In 1751, they made Lower Bengal a tributary state and conquered Orissa. The British ended their raids, however, and drove them out of Orissa in 1803. The Third Maratha War (1816-19) finally put paid to their power, and their territories from 1817 to 1853 were administered with the guidance of the British. In 1853, the last Raghuji Bhonsla died and their territories passed to the British who named them the Central Provinces in 1861. Baroda, meanwhile, had extended its power throughout Gujarat and the peninsula of Kathiawar, creating the region known as the Gaekwad. The Gaekwad Maharajas ruled this kingdom until it acceded to the Republic of India in 1949.

Madhav Rao II was born after his father had died and during the 21 years of his life, the power over the state apparatus lay in the hands of his minister, Nana Fadnavis (1742-1800). At the same time, Madhav Rao's uncle, Raghunathrao (1734-83), argued that the new young Peshwa was not really the child of Nana Saheb, claiming the office for himself. The French sided with Nana Fadnavis, while the British held with the contention of Raghunathrao which led to the First Maratha War of 1775 to 1782. It ended with the Treaty of Salbai that ceded the islands of Salsette and Elephanta, situated near Bombay, as well as a couple of other islands to Great Britain. Raghunathrao was given a pension and the young Peshwa was confirmed in his role. Aged 21, he committed suicide in 1795.

The seventh and last of these hereditary Peshwas was Baji Rao II (r. 1796-1818). He incurred the wrath of the Holkar leader when he had one of his kinsmen killed and, in 1802, Yashwantrao Holkar (r. 1807-11), ruler of Indore, defeated Baji Rao's army at the Battle of Poona. Baji Rao asked the British East India Company for protection and signed the Treaty of Bassein in 1802 that allowed for a force of British troops to safeguard him and his territories. The treaty has been described as 'the death knell of the Maratha Confederacy'.

The Maratha chieftains were disgusted by the treaty but the British had 53,000 soldiers on hand and the Second Maratha War ensued. In September 1803, the Sindhia lost to Lord Gerard Lake (1744-1808) at Delhi and to Lord Arthur Wellesley (1769-1852) – later the Duke of Wellington – at Assaye. The British continued to win, at Asirgarh Fort and at Laswari. Wellesley was victorious over the Bhonsle at Argaon in November 1803 and Holkar signed a treaty with the British. The defeated Marathas had to cede large swathes of territory to the British. This victory also led to the end of French influence in India and the restoration of the titular emperor in Delhi, although he was under British control.

A Third Maratha War followed in 1817-18 between troops of the British East India Company and the Marathas of Holkar and the Bhonsle but this one was decisive. It started with a British invasion of Maratha territory, led by Governor-General Francis Rawdon-Hastings, the Marquess of Hastings (1754-1826). It was something of a mopping-up operation after the previous conflict which the British had had to abandon due to economic difficulties. The forces of Baji Rao II, Mudhoji II Bhonsle (r. 1816-18) of Nagpur and Malhar Rao Holkar II (r. 1811-33) of Indore were assembled to meet them. It did not take long for the British to emerge victorious, finally bringing Maratha power to an end. Baji Rao surrendered himself and was sent to live on a small estate at Bithur, near Kanpur where there was a large British military presence that could keep him under surveillance. His territories were annexed to the Bombay Presidency and he died in 1851.

Bhonsle was defeated in the Battle of Sitabuldi in November 1817 and Holkar in the Battle of Mahidpur a month later. The northern part of Bhonsle's territories in and around Nagpur was annexed by British India as the Sagor and Nerbudda Territories and Indore also became part of the British domain in India. Along with Gwalior from the Sindhia and Jhansi from the Peshwa's territories, these areas all became Princely States under British control.

Chapter Seven

The Europeans

The Portuguese in India

The Portuguese explorer Vasco da Gama's 1498 discovery of the sea route to India, connecting the Atlantic and Indian Oceans and the West with the Orient had deep and lasting implications for the world. It laid the foundations for an age of global imperialism and colonial empires that enriched European nations at the expense of conquered peoples in faraway places.

Of course, Europeans were no strangers to India. The Greeks and other Mediterranean nations had travelled there long before the Portuguese and trade with India can be traced far back into history. These exploits had given Europeans a taste for the exotic, a hunger for the spices, jewels and precious metals of the East. After years of attempts to reach the Indies by sea, at great cost in terms of lives and ships, da Gama's momentous voyage gave access to the riches of the East without having to negotiate the perilous overland routes, routes that were proving even more difficult to travel because of the Ottoman Turks. It was crucial, therefore, that someone navigated around the Cape to India and Vasco da Gama and his three little caravels did just that, landing at Calicut on the Malabar Coast on 20 May 1498.

Arab sailors were unhappy with da Gama's arrival, as they had dominated the sea trade with India for centuries but the

Hindu raja of Calicut welcomed him. The Portuguese explorer remained on the Malabar Coast for six months before returning to Europe bringing with him a letter from the raja to the king of Portugal:

> 'Vasco da Gama, a nobleman of your household, has visited my kingdom and has given me great pleasure. In my kingdom there is an abundance of cinnamon, cloves, ginger, pepper and precious stones. What I seek from your country is gold, silver, coral and scarlet.'

Da Gama was welcomed home as a returning hero, his arrival celebrated every bit as much as the homecoming of Christopher Columbus from the West Indies had been celebrated by the Spanish a few years previously. Portugal dreamed of a huge overseas empire and da Gama's voyage of discovery had been undertaken with the king's patronage which made the voyage a royal enterprise rather than a national one. Ordinary Portuguese could mount commercial expeditions but they were only allowed to participate with the understanding that they would have to hand over a percentage of their profits to the king.

It was the Portuguese king's choice of Antwerp in Belgium as the city in the north in which Indian goods would be sold that led indirectly to England trading directly with India. England purchased all its goods from India in Antwerp but, when the Spanish seized the city in 1585, the trade was shut down because England was at war with Spain. Thus, the English were forced to trade directly with India.

Further expeditions left for India after Vasco da Gama's. Pedro Alvares Cabral (c. 1467 or 1468-c. 1520) established a factory, or trading post, for the purchase of goods at Calicut, and he left another at Cochin (now Kochi). On da Gama's next trip, in 1502, sailing with a fleet of 20 ships, he signed alliances with the rajas of Cochin and the rani of Quilon (now Kollam). In 1503, Alfonso de Albuquerque (*c.* 1453-1515) built a fort at Cochin and left 150 men to protect the raja who had been attacked by the *zamorin* (king) of Calicut. As soon as he left, the fort was attacked by the *zamorin* but the Portuguese defeated him on land and at sea, thus gaining the respect of the locals.

Two years later Francisco de Almeida (*c.* 1450-1510), who would be the first Portuguese viceroy of India, arrived with a force of 1,500 soldiers. He decided that, given the antipathy of Muslim traders to Portuguese factories, they should be fortified. Still, he did not want there to be too many factories, perceiving Portugal's real power to be on the sea.

There were other external problems. The new sea route was denting the coffers of the Mameluke Sultan of Egypt because the overland route through his territories was not being used as much. He sent a fleet to force the Portuguese from the area and, indeed, his admiral defeated a Portuguese fleet off Chaul, 60 kilometres south of Mumbai in 1508. The Portuguese took their revenge with a comprehensive victory near the island of Diu, off Gujarat's south coast, in 1509. This, plus the fact that the Egyptians now had to contend with the Turks, gave the Portuguese the opportunity to establish themselves in the subcontinent.

When Albuquerque took over from Almeida as governor, Portuguese policy in India changed. Albuquerque was keen to establish an empire, taking possession of strategically important locations on the coast and manipulating the local princes. In 1510, he captured Goa which remained in Portuguese hands until 1961 when it was annexed by India. He also took Malacca which gave him control of the waters of the Indian archipelago.

He opened up trade routes with Siam and the Spice Islands and sailed into the Red Sea to capture Ormuz in the Persian Gulf. Until 1600, the Portuguese enjoyed a monopoly in the spice trade, their empire in the east complemented by colonies along the west coast of Africa, and Brazil across the Atlantic.

The end of Portuguese supremacy in the East came when the Portuguese and Spanish crowns were united under Philip II (r. 1556-1598) in 1580. Portuguese interests in Asia became secondary to Spanish affairs in Europe. The union lasted until 1640 but by then the Dutch and the English had begun to take a greater interest in the East and the Portuguese were no match for their power.

The Dutch in India

The Dutch Revolt of 1566 to 1648 shut down the trade from Spanish and Portuguese ports which made the Dutch, like the English, seek their own trade with India. The first Dutchman to round the Cape of Good Hope was Jan Huyghen van Linschoten of Harlem (1563-1611) who was in Goa from 1586 to 1589. Private companies began to trade with the East and, in 1602, the Dutch government decided to unite these companies into one entity known to the Dutch as the United East Indian Company (*Vereenigde Oost-Indische Compagnie*) and to the British as the Dutch East India Company. It is often regarded as the first multinational company in history and was the first company to issue stock. In its first 50 years of existence, it established factories all over the east – in Sumatra, Ceylon, the Persian Gulf and on the coasts of the Red Sea. Its first settlement in India was at Pulicat, 20 miles to the north of Madras, which was set up in 1609. They established another outpost at Surat in 1618. A year later they built the city of Batavia (modern-day Jakarta) as the base for all their operations in the East.

At this time, the Dutch navy was the most formidable in the world. They memorably inflicted a defeat on the English at Amboyna in Indonesia in 1623, but it was this defeat that persuaded the English East India Company to relocate from the eastern archipelago to India, thereby beginning Britain's long and lucrative interest in the subcontinent. In fact, the English and the Dutch were involved in conflict until 1689 when William III of Orange (r. 1689-1702) acceded to the British throne.

In 1640, the Dutch took Malacca, to the dismay of the Portuguese, and by 1647 they were trading at Sadras on the Coromandel Coast. They established a colony at the Cape of Good Hope in 1652, as a staging post for the voyage to India, and established a factory on the Madras coast the same year. From 1661 to 1664, the Dutch seized all the Portuguese settlements south of Goa on the Malabar Coast and in 1669 they drove them out of San Thome in Madras.

The Dutch policy in the East was never a consolidated one and they failed to deal with the indigenous people effectively. The Dutch East India Company paid its employees poorly which led to a culture of corruption and callousness. Eventually, during the wars with the French between 1795 and 1811, the English seized every Dutch colony. In the Anglo-Dutch London Treaty of 1824, which was designed to solve a number of problems arising from the British occupation of Dutch possessions during the Napoleonic Wars, the Dutch ceded to Britain all their possessions in India.

The British in India – Early Years

The English had attempted to reach India by the Northwest Passage. The Genoese navigator and explorer John Cabot (*c.* 1450-*c.* 1500) tried and failed, sailing under an English flag in 1496, although he did discover the island of Newfoundland. In 1553, Sir Hugh Willoughby (?-1554) tried to find a way to India along the north of Europe and Asia, dying in the process. Others tried and similarly failed between 1576 and 1616. The first Englishman to visit India is said by some to have been Thomas Stevens (*c.* 1549-1619), a Jesuit, who arrived in Goa in 1579. In 1583, three English merchants – Ralph Fitch (*c.* 1550-1611), John Newberry, and William Leedes – and James Story, a painter, set out for Tripoli and Aleppo in Syria. From there they made their way to Baghdad and onwards to Ormuz where they were arrested as spies and sent to Goa. Thomas Stevens helped them to get out of jail after which they travelled to the court of the Mughal emperor, Akbar. Leedes, a jeweller, found gainful employment with Akbar. Fitch travelled onwards from Agra to Allahabad, joining a convoy 'of one hundred and fourscore boates laden with Salt, Opium, Hinge (asafoetida), Lead, Carpets and diverse other commodities going downe the river jumna (Yamuna) to Allahabad'. Meanwhile, Newberry decided to return home, but is believed to have been murdered in the Punjab. Fitch continued his journey, visiting much of India before returning to London in 1591. His experience proved extremely useful to the East India Company.

In 1591, the first English expedition to sail round the Cape of Good Hope and into the Indian Ocean set off. The ship *Edward Bonaventure*, captained by James Lancaster (*c.* 1554-1618), who would be one of the founders of the East India Company, visited India and other places, returning to port three years later laden with riches. But, despite the information brought back by Fitch and Lancaster, there was still no great impetus in England to develop the sea trade.

The English East India Company

In the last years of the sixteenth century, to the dismay of English merchants, the Dutch introduced a hefty increase in the price of pepper. A meeting on the subject was held in London at which merchants agreed to form an association to trade directly with India. On 31 December 1600, the English East India Company was given a royal charter to trade with the 'East Indies'. The first governor of the new company was Thomas Smith, or Smythe (c. 1558-1625).

The company sponsored 12 voyages between 1600 and 1612, all of them funded by subscribers who received all the profits at the end of each trip. Most of these journeys were extremely successful ventures, reaping profits that rarely fell below 100 per cent. The first few established trading relations in Sumatra, the Moluccas and Java as well as Banda and Amboyna. As the Company's trade spread further east to China and Japan, private merchants were attracted to the business but sometimes these went awry, as in the case of Sir Edward Michelborne (c. 1562-c. 1611), granted a licence to trade 'to Cathay, China, Japan, Corea and Cambaya' by James I in 1606. Michelborne plundered the native traders of India, disgracing the name of the East India Company and hampering future trading efforts.

The fifth venture in 1608 ran into trouble when the Dutch prevented the English merchants from trading at Banda, forcing them to go on to the Moluccas to obtain a cargo to take home. That same year, Captain William Hawkins (fl. c. 1600) travelled as an envoy of the king to the court at Agra of the

Moghul Emperor Jahangir, son of Akbar the Great, remaining there for three years. Meanwhile, the Company built a dockyard at Deptford that opened the way for bigger ships to be built for the trip round the Cape.

The sixth voyage, commanded by Sir Henry Middleton (?-1613), arrived at Cambay (now Khambhat) in Gujarat where it was attacked by the Portuguese. This did not prevent him from gaining trading concessions from the local authorities. The seventh voyage founded trading posts at Pettipollee, Nizampatam and Masulipatam. There was more trouble from the Portuguese in 1612 when the Company's ships were attacked by a large force at Surat. The English defeated them, however, which made a deep impression on the local people who had previously considered the Portuguese to be invincible. It was an incident that persuaded the Mughal emperor to give permission for the English to establish a factory at Surat which would remain the centre of the Company's operations until 1687 when it was moved to Bombay.

A decisive moment arrived in 1615 when James I sent Sir Thomas Roe (c. 1581-1644) to Jahangir's court. Sir Thomas extracted more concessions from the emperor and the prospects for English trade with India were greatly enhanced as is demonstrated by a letter that Jahangir sent to James I:

'Upon which assurance of your royal love I have given my general command to all the kingdoms and ports of my dominions to receive all the merchants of the English nation as the subjects of my friend; that in what place soever they choose to live, they may have free liberty without any restraint; and at what port soever they shall arrive, that neither Portugal nor any other shall dare to molest their quiet; and in what city soever they shall have residence, I have commanded all my governors and captains to give them freedom answerable to their own desires; to sell, buy, and to transport into their country at their pleasure. For confirmation of our love and friendship, I desire your Majesty to command your merchants to bring in their ships of all sorts of rarities and rich goods fit for my palace; and that you be pleased to send me your royal letters by every opportunity, that I may rejoice in your health and prosperous affairs; that our friendship may be interchanged and eternal.'

The Company's approach was different to that of the Portuguese. 'Quiet trade' was the objective. Factories would not be fortified and they would not be protected by garrisons. Instead, the Company relied upon the Mughals to provide protection. Only when the Marathas began to cause trouble and the Mughal Empire entered its decline did this notion become redundant. That occurred during the stewardship in Bombay of Sir John Child (?-1690), the *de facto* first Governor-General of British possessions in India.

In 1619, the English and the Dutch signed a Treaty of Defence that was designed to prevent disputes between their two trading companies, although ultimately it did little to end the animosity. Skirmishes broke out between personnel of the two companies and the Portuguese were still attacking English ships, albeit with little success. The English continued to open agencies both in India and elsewhere.

Events of 1623 persuaded the English to focus most of their attention on India. That year a contingent of English, Portuguese and Japanese sailors were executed by the Dutch at Amboyna for allegedly conspiring to attack the Dutch garrison there. There was outrage in England but, from then on, the Dutch were totally in control of the trade of Indonesia, the Malay

Peninsula and Java. They expanded their control of the spice trade in the 1660s when they forced the Portuguese out of the Malaccan Straits. The English, effectively cut off from the spice trade after Amboyna, launched a campaign of factory openings in the subcontinent. By 1647 they had 23, each managed by a governor, a master merchant or a factor and each employing 90 people. The most important of these establishments were Fort William which was located in Bengal, Fort St George, situated in Madras, and Bombay Castle.

In 1657, Oliver Cromwell renewed the East India Company's 1609 charter and, in a series of five acts around 1670, after the monarchy was restored, Charles II greatly strengthened the EIC, giving it extraordinary additional powers. It could make territorial acquisitions, mint its own money, command fortresses and troops and make alliances. It could also declare war, sue for peace and was made responsible for civil and criminal jurisdiction over any territory that it acquired.

For decades the Company battled with Parliament to make its charter more permanent, but the government was understandably unwilling to give up its share of the profits. And these were substantial. By 1712, 15 per cent of British imports came from India and almost all of those goods were handled by the Company. An act of 1730 extended the licence until 1766.

The Carnatic Wars

The main French East India Company base in India was at Pondicherry, to the south of the city of Madras. After 1742, the French operation there was led by Joseph-François Dupleix (1697-1763) who had been involved in trade in India for twenty years. Like the British in Madras, Dupleix aimed to gain influence with the rulers of a number of regional Indian states but these ambitions, plus the Austrian War of Succession, would lead to conflict – the three Carnatic Wars of 1746-49, 1751-54 and 1756-63.

Britain entered the Austrian War of Succession in 1744, on the opposite side to France. In India, however, all remained quiet and French officers were instructed to avoid conflict. No such order was given to the British and a fleet of Royal Navy ships engaged and captured a number of French vessels off the Indian coast. The French sent reinforcements, and in July 1746 French and British ships skirmished off the coast of Naggapatinam. In September that year, the French seized the British base at Madras. They promised to return it but Dupleix reneged on that promise, handing it over, instead, to Anwaruddin Khan, Nawab of Arcot (r. 1744-49). The Nawab sent a force of 10,000 men to Madras but was defeated by troops of the French East India Company at the Battle of Adyar. French efforts to capture the British Fort St David at Cuddalore in modern-day Tamil Nadu were repulsed by British reinforcements following which the British, in turn, besieged the French base at Pondicherry but had to abandon the siege when the monsoon rains arrived in October. The end of the war in Europe also brought a conclusion to the fighting in India, the Treaty of Aix-la-Chapelle returning Madras to the British.

The Second Carnatic War broke out over a succession issue in India. When Nizam-al-Mulk died in 1748, having established Hyderabad as an independent kingdom during the Mughal Empire's decline, a power struggle broke out for the position of Nawab of Arcot. The British supported Nizam-al-Mulk's son Nizam Nasir Jung (r. 1748-50) and his protégé Muhammad Ali (r. 1749-95), while the French championed the candidacy of Nizam-al-Mulk's grandson Muzaffar Jung (r. 1750-51) and Chanda Sahib (?-1752). Muzaffar and Chanda

Sahib captured Arcot and, after the death of Nasir Jung, they also took Hyderabad. But Muzaffar was killed soon after which resulted in Salabat Jung (r. 1751-62), son of Asaf Jah I, becoming Nawab. The indomitable Robert Clive (1725-74), a controversial figure who would play a major role in India, led a contingent of British troops in capturing Arcot and the war ended with the 1754 Treaty of Pondicherry that recognised Muhammad Ali as Nawab of the Carnatic. It marked the end of the road for Dupleix who was replaced by a French government anxious to sue for peace. He died in poverty and obscurity back in France.

The Third Carnatic War arose out of the Seven Years' War in Europe. This time the war spread out of the south and into Bengal. There, in 1757, British troops took the French settlement at Chandernagore (now Chandannagar). In the south, Sir Eyre Coote (1726-83) won a significant victory over the French at the Battle of Wandiwash in 1760, after which the French base at Pondicherry fell to the British. The Treaty of Paris ended the Third Carnatic War, handing back Pondicherry and Chandernagore to the French. It also permitted the French to have factories in India but French traders were prohibited from running them. The French also agreed to support British client governments. The treaty effectively ended French ambitions in India and left Britain as the most powerful European presence in the subcontinent.

Another consequence of the Carnatic Wars was that they demonstrated the effectiveness of European firepower. It took only a small infantry formation to defeat a numerically superior detachment of Indian cavalry, for instance. Military superiority would prove vital to the rise of the British East India Company.

The Black Hole of Calcutta and the Battle of Plassey

The EIC built Fort William to provide protection for its trade in Calcutta which was the main city of what would become the Bengal Presidency. ('Presidencies' were the names given to the administrative divisions of British governance in India.) Given the acrimonious situation with the French East India Company, the British had begun to reinforce the fort.

Feeling threatened by what he saw as British interference in the political situation in his territory, the local ruler, the Nawab of Bengal, Siraj ud-Daulah (r. 1756-57), demanded that they stop their reinforcement of the fort, a demand ignored by the EIC. Siraj marched on Calcutta and besieged Fort William. Seeing that the situation was hopeless, the British commander of the fort ordered his men to escape, leaving behind 146 soldiers who were under the command of John Zephaniah Holwell (1711-98), a former military surgeon who was a senior bureaucrat with the Company. They were helpless against Siraj's force, especially as the EIC's Indian troops deserted en masse, and the fort fell on 20 June 1757. Between 64 and 69 surviving British troops were taken prisoner along with those Anglo-Indian troops who had remained and a number of civilians.

Holwell met with Siraj ud-Daulah who assured him that no harm would come to the prisoners. At 8 o'clock in the evening Siraj's men locked them in the fort's prison which soldiers had nicknamed 'the black hole', a small room measuring 14 by 18 feet. The cramped conditions, the summer heat and the shock of confinement wreaked havoc overnight. At 6 o'clock the following morning, when the door was opened, only around 23 remained alive (numbers vary greatly in different accounts) of approximately 64 who had been imprisoned. It is speculated that the lower ranks of Siraj's army had effectively taken revenge as Holwell noted in his account: '[It] was the result of revenge and resentment, in the breasts of the lower *Jemmaatdaars* (sergeants), to whose custody we were delivered, for the number of their order killed during the siege.' Reportedly, the troops were imprisoned in this manner without the knowledge of Siraj ud-Daulah.

Colonel Robert Clive and Admiral Charles Watson (1714-57) marched north from Madras with a force of 3,000 troops to punish the Nawab for the incident, the two sides meeting at the Battle of Plassey which took place at Palashi about 93 miles north of Calcutta. The British had been concerned about being outnumbered but Siraj ud-Daulah's 50,000 men, 40 cannons and 10 war elephants were defeated after the Nawab fled the battlefield. Plassey is considered a significant moment in Britain's efforts to control the subcontinent. They were able to extract large concessions from Siraj and used the revenue earned from this to bolster further their military power in the region.

Following the battle, the British usurped the French position of authority in Bengal. In 1759, EIC troops defeated a numerically superior French garrison at Masulipatam, securing the Northern Circars, a narrow stretch of land lying along the western side of the Bay of Bengal. This helped to deprive the Hyderabad State of its coastline, rendering it landlocked and surrounded by British India on all sides. The Battle of Plassey is often recognised as the start of British rule in the subcontinent.

As part of an agreement between Mir Jafar (r. 1757-60, 1763-65) and the EIC, Siraj was executed following the Battle of Plassey and Mir Jafar himself became Nawab of Bengal. However, he was unhappy to be in thrall to the British and encouraged the Dutch East India Company to throw the EIC out of Bengal. Towards the end of 1759, the Dutch dispatched 7 ships and 1,400 troops from Java to Bengal, ostensibly to reinforce the settlement they had established at Chinsurah in Bengal. Clive sprang into action and attacked, defeating the much larger Dutch force in the Battle of Chinsurah on 25 November. Clive then removed Mir Jafar from the Bengali throne, installing his son-in-law Mir Qasim (r. 1761-63) as Nawab. After Qasim began to show too much of an independent spirit, Clive returned Mir Jafar to power in 1763, forcing Mir Qasim to seek the help of the Mughal emperor, Shah Alam. As has already been noted, in the Battle of Buxar in 1764, the Mughal emperor was defeated by an EIC force. Political control of Bengal was handed to an Indian official appointed by the Company but tax collecting was placed in the hands of the EIC.

By this time, suffering from ill health, Robert Clive had been forced to return to England, although he did so a wealthy man. Ennobled as Lord Clive, Baron of Plassey, in the Republic of Ireland, he won a seat in the House of Commons but there was a great deal of criticism in England of the rich ex-employees of the Company who were perceived to have plundered the riches of India and now returned to live in wealthy splendour. Clive is said to have received £234,000 in cash at Plassey and an annual allowance from India of £30,000. After Plassey, employees of the Company trading privately in Bengal were exempt from all taxes and were permitted unlimited credit.

The British East India Company was now able to install puppet governments in the various Indian states which gave employees licence to indulge in excesses, abuses of power and even atrocities in order to collect the relevant taxes. The impact upon the Indian economy was devastating. One study has concluded that India's share of world manufacturing output fell from 24.5 per cent in 1750 to just 2.8 per cent 30 years later. By 1913 it had fallen even further to 1.3 per cent and it was still only 2.4 per cent in 1938.

The Bengal Famine

In Bengal there was a partial shortfall in the harvest of 1768. This was not unusual, but the following year the weather became more extreme and by September there was a severe drought. The officials of the British East India Company began to receive reports of distress in rural areas but paid little attention to them. A few months later, in the opening months of 1770, there was serious starvation and huge numbers were dying from lack of food by the middle of the year. One British newspaper reported on the arrival of a ship from India:

> 'She brings an account of the terrible famine which has made dreadful ravages amongst the natives of Bengal; and that about two million of persons had died; so that there were not people enough left to bury the dead.'

It has been estimated that around ten million lost their lives, about a third of the population of the area in which the famines occurred. Huge parts of Bengal were depopulated by death and by people migrating from the area in search of sustenance. Much cultivated land was abandoned which quickly reverted to jungle and was out of commission for decades after. The poverty and privations engendered by the famines also led to a breakdown in law and order and gangs of bandits and Thuggee – organised gangs of professional robbers – roamed the Bengali countryside.

The EIC bore a large part of the blame for the Bengal famine. It continually increased the tax on the land, often by as much as tenfold. People were paying up to 50 per cent of the value of their agricultural produce in land tax, leaving not a great deal to live on. This was made worse by the fact that all of this revenue flowed back to Great Britain and was of no benefit to Indians. Cultivation of the opium poppy by the EIC also contributed to the situation as fields producing food crops were given over to it. The Company had a monopoly over opium cultivation in Bengal and Bihar and shipped it through middlemen to China where it was exchanged for gold and silver bullion. That bullion was used to buy Chinese goods that were then transported back for sale in England. The opium trade brought huge profits to the EIC and involved the British in two wars to enforce the Chinese government to legalise the opium trade. Although the EIC would lose its charter in 1833, opium remained a monopoly of the British government for a further 22 years, making up to 15 per cent of the Indian government's income and 30 per cent of the total value of Indian trade. Opium imports into China ended only in 1917.

Farmers were also ordered to plant indigo instead of rice and were banned from the 'hoarding' of rice. This stopped traders and farmers storing rice that would have alleviated hunger in the event of failed harvests. Furthermore, the Company had prepared no plans for such a situation.

Robert Clive, now back in England, was the butt of much of the criticism of the EIC over the Bengal famine and his political prospects were severely damaged. He was involved in discussions in Parliament about reforming the East India Company and was often called upon to defend his actions in India. In 1773, it was insinuated in Parliament that he had made his fortune at the expense of the Company and the country, but he was exonerated by the ensuing vote. Change was afoot, however, and Parliament immediately addressed new legislation

– the Regulating Act of 1773 – designed to limit the EIC's authority in the subcontinent.

'Clive of India' died in November 1774, allegedly having stabbed himself or cut his throat with a pen knife. Other sources say that he had taken an overdose of the opium that he was using to alleviate pain from gallstone problems or some other ailment.

Reforms and Regulations

The task of governing the vast territory of India was an onerous and difficult one and military and administrative costs rocketed out of control. This coincided with a depression in Europe bringing commercial stagnation and a fall in revenue from trade. The directors of the Company petitioned the government for help and the response was the Tea Act of 1773 which permitted the EIC more autonomy in running its business in the American colonies. Importantly, it exempted it from paying customs duty on imports of tea into the colonies. When news of this act became public there was outrage amongst both the colonists and those tea merchants who were not allowed the same exemption. The colonists resented not only the fact that the Company's tea would seriously undercut that of local merchants, but also that they were to be taxed by the British Parliament in which they enjoyed no representation. Protesters blocked the unloading of tea from India in three other colonies and in Boston the tea was destroyed in the incident that became known as the 'Boston Tea Party'.

In 1773, in the face of controversy over the role and performance of the East India Company, but also against resistance from the EIC lobby in Parliament and shareholders, the government introduced the Regulating Act, later commonly known as the East India Act. This clearly set out Parliament's sovereignty and ultimate control of the EIC. It separated Company and country, stipulating that the 'acquisition of sovereignty' – gaining of territory – is 'on behalf of the Crown and not in its own right'. It allowed for British India to be subject to the control of the Crown although it would be leased back to the East India Company at a cost of £40,000 for two years. The Company would retain its virtual monopoly over Indian trade but would be mandated to send a minimum amount of goods to Great Britain every year, and British judges and magistrates were to be sent to India to run legal matters. A major change was the creation of a governing Council that would have five members and would be based in Calcutta. Three of its constituents would be government-appointed, thus giving the government a controlling vote. The three Presidencies in India – Madras, Bombay and Calcutta – were to be unified under the control of the Governor-General.

The head of this Council and the first Governor-General was Warren Hastings (1732-1818) who would hold the position from 1774 to 1785. He had been Governor-General of the Presidency of Fort William and had already brought the collection of taxes in Bengal directly under the control of the EIC. Hastings was given substantial powers, even the authority to declare war if necessary, and the Council would enjoy total legislative powers in the subcontinent. Hastings abolished the position of Nawab, bringing Bengal into direct British political rule. He was not afraid to use EIC armies, protecting an ally, Oudh, from marauding Rohilla tribes. He also attacked the Marathas in the Bombay region and finally sent troops up against Hyder Ali (r. 1761-82) ruler of the southern Indian kingdom of Mysore. These were, of course, costly operations and Hastings refilled the Company coffers by forcing the kingdoms of Oudh and

Benares to pay more tribute. Initially, the directors of the EIC were content with the stipulations of the Regulating Act but the biannual payment proved ultimately to be burdensome and contributed to a steady fall in profits.

1784 saw another act, known as Pitt's India Act. In order to separate the commercial and political activities of the Company and to ensure that it was subordinate to the British government, a Board of Commissioners for the Affairs of India – the Board of Control – was created. This bill also created a centralised British administration of the subcontinent but, when Warren Hastings was informed of the details of the act, he resigned. On his return home, Parliament brought impeachment proceedings against him, based on claims that he had extorted money from Indian allies of the EIC. The issue really at stake was whether or not the behaviour of officials that would be viewed as immoral or unethical in Britain should also be perceived as immoral in India. Nonetheless, after seven long years, Hastings was exonerated, although left almost bankrupt. The East India Company helped him out, providing him with compensation of £4,000 a year.

Other acts followed, further delineating the borders between the Crown and the Company. In 1793, the EIC's charter was extended by a further twenty years.

Lord Cornwallis

Hastings was followed as Governor-General in 1875 by Charles Cornwallis, 1st Marquess Cornwallis (1738-1805) who would occupy the position until 1793. Cornwallis was one of the leading British generals in the American War of Independence, a man of considerable moral rectitude whose remit was the reform of the EIC's Indian operations. He created what became known as the Cornwallis Code, a body of legislation enacted in 1793 to improve British governance of its Indian possessions. It dealt with policing and judicial and civil administration but it is remembered primarily for the Permanent Settlement (also known as the *zamindari* system) which introduced a tax collection scheme that lasted into the twentieth century.

Corrupt officials were not tolerated and the Company's employees were prohibited from their lucrative private trade. Indian civilians were barred from senior positions in the Company and Indian soldiers were not allowed promotion to commissioned ranks. Regional Indian judges were replaced by British judges and *zamindars* took responsibility for the collection and payment of taxes. *Zamindars* were treated as landowners, as long as they paid their taxes on time. It was a clever move, providing Company officials with a landed class that had a real interest in supporting them. The downside of this apparently clever decision was that several years of poor crops forced some *zamindars* to transfer ownership of their land to moneylenders in Calcutta.

Paramount Power

With Britain and France embroiled in wars at the end of the eighteenth and into the early nineteenth century, there was more leeway to pursue dreams of empire in India. Thus did governors-general from 1798 until 1828 indulge in warfare, annexation and alliances that were focused on making Great Britain the dominant power in the subcontinent. Richard Wellesley, then the 2nd Earl of Mornington, was dispatched to India in 1798, his principal task being to remove every last vestige of the French from the subcontinent. If it was Robert Clive who started the British ascendancy in India and Warren

Hastings who consolidated it, it was Wellesley who transformed it into an empire. His time as Governor-General was a period of rapid expansion of British power.

His first challenge involved Tipu Sultan (r. 1782-99), ruler of the Kingdom of Mysore. His father Hyder Ali had been an unyielding foe of the British and his son was no different. Hyder Ali had defeated the Company's troops in 1769 in the First Anglo-Mysore War. In 1780, in alliance with the Marathas and the Nizam of Hyderabad, he had launched the actions of the Second Anglo-Mysore war. In March 1784, Warren Hastings was ordered by the British government to secure peace after Britain and France had ended hostilities in Europe and the Treaty of Mangalore ended hostilities. By now Tipu Sultan was the ruler of Mysore and he had entered into an alliance with France. Anticipating trouble, Wellesley immediately ordered his troops to prepare for war. Supported by alliances with the Marathas and Hyderabad, he invaded Mysore in February 1799, bringing the campaign to a swift conclusion with the seizure of Seringapatam on 4 May, during which action Tipu Sultan lost his life. The Mysore kingdom was divided between the winners and the half of the territory that went to the EIC gave it direct access from Madras to the west coast of India. Wellesley put a Hindu on the throne of what was left of Mysore and signed a subsidiary alliance with him. By this arrangement, rulers would be protected by EIC troops in return for ceding to the Company all rights to manage their states' external affairs. They paid for a contingent of British troops and a Company official to reside at their courts and while the ruler was responsible for all domestic matters, the Company controlled all foreign affairs, including decisions about when to go to war or when to negotiate for peace.

In the next two years, Wellesley annexed a number of

territories from rulers with whom the Company had been allied for some time – Tanjore in 1799, Surat in 1800 and 1801, Nellore, the Carnatic and Trichonopoly. The Nawab of Oudh was persuaded to abdicate and in negotiations for a subsidiary alliance, Wellesley annexed two-thirds of the territory.

The Second Maratha War, in which Wellesley's brother Arthur – later the Duke of Wellington – played such an important role, was the result of the restoration to the position of Peshwa of Baji Rao II. Ultimately, Wellesley achieved the desired result and the French influence in India was extinguished. Baji Rao II signed a subsidiary alliance and Wellesley used this treaty to justify assaults on the four Maratha clans in the Deccan. By 1805, he had signed similar agreements with the Bhonsle and Sindhia as well as Orissa and the cities of Delhi and Agra, all of which the Marathas had controlled. The EIC added forty million people and tens of millions of pounds in revenue to its treasury. Further to this, he used the 'subsidiary alliance' to gain even more territories for Britain.

The power of the Marathas and all the other princes and rulers was gone and the British had India to themselves. Wellesley left, having turned the East India Company into an imperial power, leaving behind a grand new Government House in Calcutta but saying in defence of the expense of such a construction project:

'I wish India to be ruled from a palace, not from a counting-house; with the ideas of a Prince, not with those of a retail-dealer in muslins and indigo.'

Chapter Eight

Consolidating Empire: 1805-57

Governors-General

Wellesley's activities were extremely costly, leading to his replacement by Lord Cornwallis, who returned to the post in 1805. Within ten weeks of arriving in the subcontinent, however, he was dead, his task of bringing peace at any price unfulfilled. He was succeeded by Sir George Barlow (1763-1846) as acting Governor-General. He had been a close adviser to Sir John Shore (1751-1834) who had been Governor-General from 1793-97 and to Wellesley. At this time Holkar and Sindhia were still unsubdued and Barlow left the Rajput chiefs at their mercy. There was a mutiny of the Madras Sepoys (soldiers) at Vellore in 1806 over the type of turban that could be worn and the banning of caste marks while in uniform. It was quickly subdued but was a shock to the empire.

Gilbert Elliot, Baron Minto of Minto (1751-1814) replaced Barlow in 1807. A Scottish politician and diplomat, Minto was successful in preventing too much violence in central India which remained restless. His orders were non-intervention. The Earl of Moira – later Marquess of Hastings – followed him. As Francis Rawdon-Hastings, he had served with the British forces in the American War of Independence and was a close friend of the Prince of Wales, later George IV (r. 1820-30).

He completed the conquests of Wellesley in central India and his long term of office, from 1813 to 1823 included two major conflicts – a campaign against the Gurkhas of Nepal and the last war with the Marathas. As we have already seen, the conclusion of the Maratha War ended all open resistance to the British.

Lord Amherst (1773-1857) succeeded the Marquess of Hastings in 1823, remaining in office until 1828. A former ambassador to China, Amherst was fairly inexperienced and was heavily influenced by senior British military officers in Bengal. His five years as Governor-General are notable for the annexation of Assam that led to the First Burmese War and the taking of Bharatpur.

The war with Burma lasted two years and was fought over a territorial dispute that turned violent in September 1823. 15,000 British troops lost their lives and the war cost £13 million, leading to an economic crisis in British India. Amherst was lucky not to be recalled in shame at the war's conclusion but he had influential friends such as George Canning and the Duke of Wellington. He was replaced in 1828 by an acting Governor-General, William Butterworth Bayley (1782-1860), before Lord William Bentinck (1774-1839), a former soldier and serving Member of Parliament, was given the job, holding it until 1833.

Bentinck's immediate task was to restore the finances devastated by the Burmese War. He made reductions in annual costs of around one and a half million pounds, including cuts in soldiers' wages which earned him the enmity of those serving in India. He also ensured that there was revenue from land that had not yet been assessed and placed duties on opium. He made English the language of the courts instead of Persian and promoted Western-style education for Indians so that more educated Indians would be available for work in the bureaucracy.

Controversially, Bentinck introduced legislation to curb the practice of *sati*, with the Bengali Sati Regulation of 1829. He also tried to restrict other Indian practices that were offensive to Western sensibilities with the help of the controversial social reformer, Raja Ram Mohan Roy (1772-1833). Known as the 'Father of Modern India', Roy was the founder, in 1828, of the Brahmo Subha movement that led to the influential socio-religious movement Brahmo Samaj.

An Administrative Body

In 1833, during Bentinck's tenure, the charter was again renewed, until 1853, but with conditions. The Government of India Act 1833 was passed against the background of the Industrial Revolution and the rise of the economic ideology of 'laissez-faire'. According to this economic theory, transactions between private parties should be free from government interference in the form of regulations, privileges, tariffs and subsidies. It greatly changed the operations of the East India Company. The Act took away the Company's remaining trade monopolies and the Governor-General title – until then Governor-General of Bengal – was changed to Governor-General of India. The Governor-General's Government now became the 'Government of India' and his council the 'India Council'. The Governor-General and his executive council now assumed legislative powers for all of India under British control. Crucially, the British East India Company's operation as a commercial entity was ended which transformed it into an administrative body. It lost its trade with China and other parts of the Far East.

After a year of an acting Governor-General, George Eden, Lord Auckland (1784-1849) took the reins. A former First

Lord of the Admiralty, Auckland held office from 1836 to 1842. He became preoccupied with problems in Afghanistan in 1838 after he tried to install Shah Shuja on the throne of Kabul which resulted in the massacre of the British garrison there. In 1842, as the debacle in Afghanistan proceeded, he was replaced by Edward Law, Lord Ellenborough (1790-1871) who was given the job of restoring peace to Asia. Unfortunately, however, his entire term of office – from 1842 to 1844 – was taken up with war. There were sieges at Ghazni and Jalalabad while, in Madras, the sepoys were ripe for mutiny. His plan, as stated in a memo to The Queen on 15 March 1842, was to inflict a decisive blow on the Afghans before leaving them to govern themselves. He was initially reluctant to commit to more than withdrawals from Kandahar and Ghazni but two British armies under Generals Sir George Pollock (1786-1872) and Sir William Nott (1782-1845) decided to do so by way of Kabul. In September 1842 they blew up the city's great bazaar as punishment for the massacre, freed British prisoners and marched triumphantly back to India.

Two further wars occurred during Ellenborough's tenure. Sir Charles Napier (1782-1853) defeated the Muslim rulers of Sind, reportedly sending a dispatch announcing his victory that featured just one word – 'peccavi', Latin for 'I have sinned'. The Battle of Miani in which 12,000 Baluchis were defeated by just 3,000 British troops is one of the greatest moments of the British experience in India. That same year, a succession dispute at Gwalior led to British victories against the Sindhia family in battles at Maharajpur and Panniar.

Lord Ellenborough was withdrawn in 1844, his style of administration disliked by the directors of the EIC. His replacement was a veteran soldier who had become an MP, Lieutenant-General Sir Henry Hardinge (1785-1856). He arrived in India as people began to think it would be just a matter of time before there was a trial of strength between the British and the only Hindu power that remained in India – the Sikhs.

Sikhism and the Sikh Empire

Sikhism is a monotheistic religion that emerged in the fifteenth century in the Punjab region, the term 'Sikh' deriving from the Sanskrit words for disciple or student and instruction. It was founded by Guru Nanak (1469-1539) who was born into a Hindu family in the village of Talwandi (now Nankana Sahib) which is located near Lahore. He had an enquiring mind and was fascinated by the Hindu religion as a child. At the age of 13, however, when it was time for him to be invested with the sacred thread according to the traditional Hindu custom, he refused to accept it from the Hindu priest, singing the following:

'Let mercy be the cotton, contentment the thread, Continence the knot and truth the twist. O priest! If you have such a thread, do give it to me. It'll not wear out, nor get soiled, nor burnt, nor lost. Says Nanak, blessed are those who go about wearing such a thread.'

Leaving home, he found work in Sultanpur and one day when he was 30 years old, is said to have gone to the river to bathe and meditate. He was gone for three days and on his return seemed to be 'filled with the spirit of God'. He said: 'There is no Hindu, there is no Muslim,' and with this as his message, he began missionary work, making four journeys – called *Udasis* – in the four directions, covering many thousands of miles and preaching. He appointed a new Sikh guru before he died on 22 September, 1539, aged 70.

Sikh political history can be viewed as beginning with the martyrdom of the fifth leader, Guru Arjan Dev, in 1606, and Sikh religious practices were formalised in 1699 by Guru Gobind Singh, the tenth incumbent of the role. He was responsible for the introduction of the Sikh warrior community, the *Khalsa*, and for the Five Ks, the five articles of faith that Sikhs must wear at all times. These are *Kesh* (uncut hair), *Kangha* (a wooden comb for the hair), *Kara* (a metal bracelet), *Kachera* (a type of undergarment) and *Kirpan* (a dagger).

Several Sikh gurus lost their lives at Mughal hands for refusing to convert to Islam. They also opposed the religious persecution of minority religious communities by the Islamic administration, persecution that included the Sikhs. Subsequently, the Sikhs militarised to fight the Mughals, and the Sikh Confederacy was formed of the *misls* – sovereign aristocratic republics – during the eighteenth century. In 1799, the Maharajah Ranjit Singh (*r.* 1801-39) – popularly known as *Sher-i-Punjab* (Lion of the Punjab) – managed to unite the *misls*, take over some other small local kingdoms and found the Sikh Empire. He defeated numerous invasions from Afghanistan and established cordial relations with the British.

The First Sikh War

Following the death of Ranjit Singh in 1839, the empire was beset by internal division and political mismanagement. His two sons died suspiciously, leaving two factions vying for power in the Punjab – the Sikh Sindhanwalias and the Hindu Dogras. Sher Singh (*r.* 1841-43), a Dogra, took the throne in January 1841 and senior Sindhanwalias fled for safety to British territory. The

Army of the Punjab rapidly increased in numbers and claimed to be the embodiment of the Sikh nation. Sikhs made up the executive, military and civil authority within the state, leading British observers to describe the Punjab as a 'dangerous military democracy'. British residents in the state told of Sikh soldiers running riot, killing anyone who spoke Persian, the language of officials and bureaucrats.

Although he spent fortunes on his lavish court, Maharajah Sher Singh was unable to pay his army, leading to unrest and in September 1843, his cousin, an army officer, murdered him. The Dogras took terrible revenge on those responsible and put Sher Singh's young son Duleep Singh (r. 1843-49) on the throne with his mother, the Maharani Jind Kaur (1817-63), acting as regent.

Following the death of Ranjit Singh, the EIC had begun to increase its military presence in the areas next to the Punjab, establishing a military base at Ferozepur, just a few miles from the border. Suspicion of the British increased in the Punjab following their annexation of Sind, to the south of the Punjab. For the British, however, under the Governor-Generalships of Lord Ellenborough and Sir Henry Hardinge, the Sikh army represented a serious threat to their possessions along the border. Indian and Sikh historians counter this with an argument that the British military build-up along the frontier was nothing other than offensive in nature. Of course, not only was the Sikh kingdom the last remaining stronghold in India not under British control, it was also very wealthy, and such treasures as the fabulous Koh-i-Noor diamond were kept in its treasuries. However, if war had not broken out, it is unlikely that the British would have annexed the Punjab as they did not have the military manpower to hold on to the territory.

Tension built until diplomatic relations were severed and

in late 1845 an EIC force, commanded by General Sir Hugh Gough (1779-1869), Commander-in-Chief of the Bengal Army, set out for Ferozepur to bolster the troops already there. Hardinge, the Governor-General, was with him. The Sikh army began crossing the River Sutlej on 11 December. Although they claimed they were on their own territory, the area was disputed and the British, regarding their advance as hostile, declared war. The Battle of Mudki on 18 December ended in an untidy British victory and a few days later, EIC troops won a hard-fought victory at Ferozeshah. Towards the end of January 1846, they won again at Aliwal. Finally, in the Battle of Sobraon on 10 February, the Sikh army was wiped out, British troops displaying little mercy.

In the Treaty of Lahore of March 1846, the Sikh kingdom was forced to cede to the British the valuable region of the Jullundar (now Jalandhar) Doab situated between the Beas and the Sutlej rivers and an indemnity of 15 million rupees was imposed. The Sikhs were unable to pay this sum and they were forced to hand over the areas of Kashmir, Hazarah and territories in the hill countries between the Beas and Indus rivers. Duleep Singh was permitted to remain as ruler of the Punjab with his mother as regent but the government of the Punjab requested that the British remain until the boy reached the age of 16. The Maharani was replaced by a British resident in Lahore who presided over a Council of Regency. In other words, the East India Company was now the government of the Punjab.

Modernising British India

In 1848, Hardinge was replaced by the Earl of Dalhousie (1812-60). To many, he was a far-sighted Governor-General who consolidated East India Company rule in the subcontinent, established the foundations of its later administration and, by so doing, helped to create stability for his successors. His critics, however, view him as pursuing reckless policies that did untold financial damage to the East India Company and also endangered its military hold on India. They believe he created a situation that made the Indian Rebellion of 1857 an inevitability and ultimately set the EIC on a path that would lead to it becoming a colonial administration that bled money. The high-minded and authoritarian Dalhousie has also been denigrated for his overbearing attitude, his mission to centralise all activity and for his policy of annexation.

He was interested in improving both the moral and the material state of British India but his policies were unpopular with many sections of Indian society and he had been in the job only a couple of months when the Second Sikh War broke out. It resulted from growing resentment with the British presence in the Punjab and ended with the annexation of the Punjab as the North-West Frontier Province by the EIC. Dalhousie tried to dismantle local rule in the Punjab but those who ruled – described by one source as 'audacious, eccentric, and often Evangelical pioneers' had to be replaced by Dalhousie with what he believed to be a better administrative system. The region was divided into districts – run by District Officers – and divisions – managed by Commissioners.

One of the most controversial policies introduced by Dalhousie in India was the Doctrine of Lapse which was aimed at advancing his expansionist bent by annexing any non-British state where there was no proper male heir following the death of a ruler. Employing this policy, he annexed Satara, Jaipur and Sambalpur in 1849 and he again used it to annex Jhansi and Nagpur in 1853. These were all approved by the British government although his proposed annexation of Karauli was not allowed in 1849 and two states that he annexed in 1851 and 1852 respectively – Baghat and Udaipur – were later returned to native rule. Critics think these annexations placed an unnecessary burden on the finances of the EIC.

Meanwhile, he worked hard to develop a new infrastructure for British India. Bengal, ruled for a long time by a Governor-General, was placed under the control of a Lieutenant-Governor in 1854. Military boards were abolished and selection replaced seniority in higher commands, ensuring the right calibre of people got the top positions. A department of works was created in each Presidency and engineering colleges were opened. Dalhousie had the 445-miles long Ganges Canal constructed, opening in 1854. It was built principally to provide irrigation for famine-prevention but was also used for navigation. This had the unintended result of increasing the population and no plans were in place for immunisation of this larger population or for providing educational institutions to help them improve their lot. Thus were the poor kept poor and tied to the land where they were often exploited.

The first Indian railway opened to traffic in 1853 between Bombay and Thane but the introduction of rail transport was not really aimed at benefitting Indians. Rather, it was designed to provide a means of carrying large quantities of natural resources such as coal from mining and agricultural areas inland to the Indian coast from where they could be put on ships for transportation to Britain. The railway, of which by the turn of the century there would be about 25,000 miles, can be viewed as probably the only major investment that Britain made in India.

Dalhousie also championed steam communication with Britain by way of the Red Sea and a monthly steamer service around the Cape began in 1845. He introduced the electric telegraph and cheap postage, creating a post office network. He worked tirelessly, even up to his retirement when he was in poor health, annexing Oudh in February 1856 and retiring a month later.

The Indian Rebellion of 1857

By 1857, there were more than 300,000 sepoys – local soldiers, mostly Muslim and Hindu – in the East India Company's army and there were around 50,000 British troops. Each of the three Presidencies had its own armies. The Madras and Bombay armies recruited locally and caste was unimportant. The Bengal army, on the other hand, sought its recruits from higher castes. This was partly because many of the sepoys from Bengal had fought against the EIC at Plassey and Buxar and, as a result, could not be trusted. This forced Warren Hastings to recruit from further west which took him to the areas of Bihar and Awadh and the higher castes, a practice that prevailed for the ensuing 75 years. The East India Company tried to accommodate the requirements of these men. They were allowed to dine separately and were not required to serve overseas. Hindu festivals were also acknowledged by the army.

As the EIC became bigger and more powerful, however, there were changes that angered the sepoys. They were expected to serve far from home, in places such as Burma, and were not given the extra pay for such service that had formerly been their right. In July 1856, Dalhousie introduced the General Service Enlistment Act. Until then the burden of serving in Burma and China had fallen unfairly on the two smaller Presidency armies. This new act required new recruits to accept a commitment to general service which meant serving abroad. Troops already in service, however, believed this to be just the thin end of the wedge, and that soon they too would have this requirement extended to them. Sons often followed fathers into the army and this new stipulation would fall upon them. Other factors in their disillusionment included the growing number of European officers in the armies. This made advancement through the ranks even slower for them.

The ammunition for the new Enfield P-53 rifle was another bone of contention. These used paper cartridges that were covered in grease. In order to prepare them for firing, a sepoy had to bite open the paper surrounding the cartridge to release the powder. Rumours began to spread that the grease used included tallow derived from beef, which was offensive to Hindus, and pork, which was offensive to Muslims. When the disquiet became evident to the British they stopped production and an order went out that no grease was to be used on the bullets, that the sepoys could grease them themselves using whatever they chose. There was a further amendment that allowed them to tear the paper instead of biting through it. Sepoys then claimed that the rumours must have been true and that the grease had been animal fat.

There was also unrest amongst the civilian population – nobles, rural landlords (*taluqdars*) and peasants alike. The nobles were aghast at the Doctrine of Lapse which overturned centuries of tradition in terms of inheritance. The *taluqdars* had suffered in the land reforms that had followed the annexation of Oudh, losing their lands to peasant farmers. They had also been victims of punitive land-revenue assessments that had driven them into the clutches of moneylenders or had caused them to lose their land. Cultural changes instituted by the EIC, such as the abolition of *sati* and the new law that allowed widows to re-marry, also created a suspicion amongst many Indians that the

British were trying to interfere with their religious practices and beliefs.

On Sunday 10 May 1857, sepoys based at Meerut, 35 miles northeast of Delhi openly mutinied, storming through the cantonments and killing every European they encountered. With many civilians joining their ranks, they set out for Delhi Fort where they invited Bahadur Shah II (r. 1837-57), the Mughal emperor, to lead the rebellion. He reluctantly agreed, offering his public support for the uprising. The revolt spread across North India and was joined by many leaders of the various royal families.

The British were initially slow to react, but when they did move it was decisively and with large numbers of troops, even bringing in regiments from the Crimean War. Regiments en route for China were diverted to the subcontinent. They marched on Delhi, laying siege to the city from 1 July until 31 August when the British re-took the city. Their retribution was terrible. An anonymous letter about the British capture of Delhi was published in the *Bombay Telegraph* in September 1857:

'All the city people found within the walls when our troops entered were bayoneted on the spot; and the number was considerable, as you may suppose, when I tell you that in some houses forty and fifty people were hiding. These were not mutineers, but residents of the city, who trusted to our well-known mild rule for pardon. I am glad to say they were disappointed.'

There were decisive actions at Kanpur where 120 British women and children were massacred by the sepoys and at Lucknow where there was a prolonged defence of the Residency – the British political office of the city – from June until November. There was also an important battle at Gwalior in which the Rani of Jhansi (1828-58) was killed. The rebellion was over shortly after this, although some guerrilla fighting continued until the first months of 1859.

Bahadur Shah was sent into exile at Rangoon (now Yangon) in Burma where he died in 1862. He was the last Mughal Emperor and his dynasty ended with his death.

The most important outcome of the Indian Rebellion of 1857, however, was the end of the EIC after two and a half centuries. The British government withdrew the Company's right to rule India in November 1858 and Queen Victoria's pronouncement of this was read out at every station in India.

'When, by the blessing of Providence, internal tranquillity shall be restored, it is our earnest desire to stimulate the peaceful industry of India, to promote works of public utility and improvement, and to administer its government for the benefit of all our subjects resident therein. In their prosperity will be our strength, in their contentment our security, and in their gratitude our best reward.'

In future the British government would rule directly through its representative, the Governor-General. All treaties that the Company had made with native princes would be honoured; there would be no more annexations; there would be a general amnesty for all rebels apart from those who had been involved in the murder of Europeans; all religions would be tolerated and ancient Indian customs would be respected. A reorganisation of the army followed in which the number of Indian soldiers was reduced from 200,000 to 140,000 and the number of European soldiers was raised to 65,000. Regiments were constituted in such a way that soldiers from one region were not grouped together and recruitment moved from the United Provinces and Bihar to the Punjab and the hill regions, introducing many more Sikh and Gurkha recruits. The Governor-General, Charles Canning, became Viceroy, and read Victoria's proclamation out from a platform at a grand durbar (Persian for a grand court occasion) in Allahabad. India became part of the British Empire and Queen Victoria assumed the title Empress of India in 1876.

Chapter Nine

Crown Rule: 1858 to 1905

Governing India after the East India Company

Almost a third of India was controlled by Indian princes but their rule was carefully supervised by local British residents. There were between 500 and 600 of these 'Princely States' and they ranged in size from areas as large as England to territories that covered only a few square miles. Their rulers were amongst the most supportive of British rule in the subcontinent. A number of former rulers were restored to their positions and there were assurances that the treaty obligations of the British would be rigorously observed. The British controlled the external affairs of the Princely States while internal matters were in the hands of the ruler, although even in those areas British influence could be extensive. Aristocrats and princes would form the backbone of British rule in India.

The Princely States were managed by the Viceroy and the rest of the subcontinent was governed directly by him with the counsel of a five-member Executive Council. This could be increased to 12 to create a Legislative Council that would pass new laws. Half the members of this body were British officials and permitted to vote; the other half consisted of Indians and British people resident in India who served only in an advisory capacity. The Viceroy was responsible to the Secretary of

State for India in London and, through him, to Parliament. The army and the provincial governments were all under the Viceroy's control. At the level of the districts, the Indian Civil Service handled administrative business and, after 1853, civil servants had to pass competitive examinations before receiving an appointment. The 'district magistrate' or 'collector' was in charge of each district.

In London, meanwhile, the Government of India Act 1858 allowed for a Cabinet-level Secretary of State for India and a fifteen-member Council of India, all with Indian experience. The Secretary of State was required in most instances to consult the Council, especially on matters relating to the spending of Indian revenues.

Growth and Expansion

The second half of the nineteenth century saw India's economy grow and its rural regions began to be exploited by the imperial authorities. British companies invested £150 million into the railway, roads and canals and improvements in irrigation brought an increase in land under cultivation in a number of regions. There was a dramatic increase in the Punjab where the use of canals resulted in an extra 3 million acres being cultivated by 1885. By 1947 there were an additional 14 million acres under cultivation. By the end of the nineteenth century, railways and improved road communication were making a huge difference to the transportation of goods from inland areas to the coast and also to the carrying of goods imported from Britain. In 1869, the Suez Canal was opened, making it even easier for goods to be transported and for Britain to exploit its empire more fully.

The end of the EIC's trading monopoly in 1833 had encouraged entrepreneurs to create businesses in India and many established tea and coffee estates in the east and the south of the country. These expanded rapidly and by 1871 tea plantations in Assam and in the Nilgiri Hills were exporting more than six million pounds of tea per year. By 1900, 68,500 tons of tea were being exported to Britain, India supplanting China as the country's major tea supplier.

Jute produced in eastern Bengal was transported to mills in Calcutta. The jute industry had developed in response to Russia's involvement in the Crimean War. That war cut off the supply of Russian raw hemp to the jute mills of Dundee, and caused leading producers to turn to Calcutta. In 1863, there were just two jute mills in Bengal; by 1882, there were twenty, employing more than 20,000 workers. Indigo was produced in Bihar and Bengal but, after European owners took over, workers were treated very badly. This led to India's first industrial action – a strike in 1859-60 known as the Blue Mutiny. Meanwhile, opium exports plunged as the ban on its trade came into effect and, having represented 30 per cent of all Indian exports in the 1860s, by 1920 it had disappeared completely.

India's main exports between 1860 and 1920 were raw cotton, wheat, oilseeds, jute and tea. These were – apart from tea – indigenous crops that were produced by peasant communities as part of a crop cycle. The largest export item was raw cotton which had previously been exported to China but now found new markets in Europe and Japan. Indian wheat became increasingly important. About 17 per cent of Indian cultivation was exported and it came to represent 18 per cent of British wheat imports.

A great deal of the profits of these industries went into British pockets and British bank accounts. Indian exports were controlled by British firms and they also handled the shipping and insurance of the commodities. Indian traders, middlemen and moneylenders profited, as they helped the crops to be produced but the ones who benefitted least were, of course, the peasant farmers. The highs and lows of export prices that were a result of being part of a global market hit them hard and, towards the end of the nineteenth century, many were burdened by large debts. To make matters worse, their methods were still medieval, with bullocks, wooden ploughs and carts still in use.

The British Raj

The number of long-term British residents – known as 'Anglo-Indians' – was never large. Even at the zenith of the British Empire, they probably numbered little more than 100,000. The men worked at the top end of the Indian government and the Indian Civil Service and often their families had a long connection with the subcontinent going back for generations. This made them determined that British rule in India would continue. They stuck rigidly to their limited community, eating, socialising and worshipping only with other Anglo-Indians and marrying only them or people from Britain.

Initially the journey to India had been so long and difficult that women did not accompany their husbands, leading many EIC employees to have Indian mistresses. As the journey time grew shorter, with firstly a land route across Egypt and then the opening of the Suez Canal reducing the journey time to just three weeks, more Englishwomen began to arrive, contributing to the emergence of Anglo-Indian society. British settlements were carefully separated from Indian dwellings. 'Civil Lines' were the sections set apart for Anglo-Indian and European families, and within these would be the church, polo grounds and the cemetery.

Many Anglo-Indians did good work and had a real understanding of the country in which they had chosen to live but they were often racist in their attitudes to Indian people and convinced of the superiority of the British and their way of life. They believed that Britain was engaged in a mission to civilise India, to replace its outmoded customs and way of life with the more 'advanced' culture of Great Britain and the West.

There was a great deal of movement, officers and their families regularly moving from station to station during a career and it became the practice in the 1830s for officials and their staff to relocate to hill stations during the hot Indian summer. The central government, for example, moved to the town of Simla in the Himalayas, Darjeeling was the summer destination for the Bengali provincial government and for Bombay Mahabaleshwar was the place. And life was strictly proscribed according to rigid social etiquette. Dress codes often operated and seating at a dinner party was defined by printed 'civil lists'. The Anglo-Indians were deeply conservative and this probably hindered the introduction of much-needed constitutional reforms at the turn of the century.

Imperialism, of course, proved anathema to many Indians and having been trained in an English-style system, an educated elite in the subcontinent began to think about freeing their country from what they viewed as greed and racism. The racial arrogance of the British was one more legacy of the 1857 rebellion. British excesses after the mutiny were not condemned; the focus was upon Indian excesses. Monuments to the British dead were erected but, as Jawaharlal Nehru (1889-1964) noted in 1945, 'There is no memorial for the Indians who died.' In fact, racial discrimination became institutionalised in the army and the civil service, and Indians were not promoted to positions of responsibility. In the army, for instance, there were no Indian commissioned officers until after the First World War. Nehru also said:

'The future historians of England will have to consider how far England's decline from her proud eminence was due to her imperialism and racialism, which corrupted her public life and made her forget the lessons of her own history and literature.'

Thus did educated, embittered Indians begin to organise themselves politically and launch the long struggle for self-determination.

Reform Movements

Indian pride was seriously dented by the imperialism and racism of the British. Coupled with the dissemination of Western ideas and culture through education, it gave rise to a variety of religious and social reform movements. These would presage the nationalist movements that emerged during the early years of the twentieth century.

The monotheistic Brahmo Samaj (Society of Brahma) had been founded in Bengal, as we have seen, by Ram Mohun Roy in 1828 as the Brahma Saba and was the most influential of the early reform movements. It was led in the second half of the nineteenth century, until his death in 1905, by Debendranath Tagore (1817-1905) – son of Dwarkanath (1794-1846) and father of Rabindranath (1861-1941) – and Keshab Chandra Sen (1838-84). Its membership was made up of mostly high-caste Hindu intellectuals who knew something of Western thought and Christianity. The Brahmo Samaj was opposed to idol worship and caste but still accepted that Brahmos were Hindus.

The Ramakrishna Mission took its message from the mystic Ramakrishna Paramahamsa. It was led by Swami Vivekananda (1863-1902), who had been educated at Calcutta University, and who had toured the United States where he had been very well received. He preached a Vedantic philosophy that was based on the *Upanishads* and also encouraged Indians to change Hindu social practices. He introduced Yoga to the West and is often credited with bringing Hinduism to the status of a major world religion.

The Arya Samaj emerged in the Punjab, founded in 1875 by the Hindu ascetic, Dayananda Saraswati (1824-83). His catchphrase was 'Back to the Vedas' and he worked for a society in which caste was no longer a factor and there was no more worship of idols, multiple gods, temples or elaborate rituals. He claimed that anything that needed to be known could be found in the Vedas – even recent Western technological developments such as the railway. The Arya Samaj was vehemently anti-Christian and sought to convert Indians from other religions to Hinduism.

In Maharashtra there were social reform movements such as the Satyasodhak Samaj (Society of Truth-seekers) that was founded in 1873 by Jyotirao Phule (1827-90) in order to fight oppression by the Brahmins. Phule founded schools for girls and Untouchables and an orphanage. His work marked the beginning of the anti-Brahmin political movement in Maharashtra and the movement there on behalf of the Untouchables that was led by B. R. Ambedkar (1891-1956).

Indian Muslims also moved for reform. Following the demise of the Mughal Empire, they found themselves increasingly disadvantaged. The Aligarh movement was established to encourage Muslims to embrace modern ideas. It began at the Muhammadan Anglo-Oriental College (later the Aligarh Muslim

129

University) in Aligarh, founded by scholar and jurist Sir Syed Ahmad Khan (1817-98) who had enjoyed close relationships with both the Mughal court and the East India Company. His college, the first Muslim English language college in India, was established along the lines of Cambridge University and his initial objective was to teach Muslim students English and science. As he wrote at the time:

'The adoption of a new system of education does not mean the renunciation of Islam. It means its protection... The truth of Islam will shine the more brightly if its followers are well educated, familiar with the highest in the knowledge of the world; it will come under an eclipse if its followers are ignorant.'

Later, he founded the Muhammadan Educational Conference that would lead to the establishment of the political party, the All-India Muslim League after his death.

Women in Nineteenth-Century India

For many British who were critical of Indian society and culture, the social condition of women was an exemplar of its backwardness. Men educated in the West began to debate some of the practices that seemed distasteful to modern sensibilities, such as child marriage, purdah (the seclusion of women), the proscription of re-marriage for widows and the Hindu religion's prohibition of women being able to access literacy and education.

During the second half of the nineteenth century, societies were founded to encourage education and social reform for women and amongst the urban elites more women began to benefit from education. By 1927, there were two million girls in education. Of course, this was just a tiny percentage of the female population of India, but it was an advance. In the middle of the nineteenth century it was fairly rare in a province such as Bengal for a woman to have received any education; by the start of the twentieth century, education was the norm for an urban middle-class girl. Much else changed. The age at which women were married rose, women were seen in public a great deal more than previously and widow re-marriage was slightly more acceptable.

The men educated in the Western style were eager for their wives to be modern, literate and educated, and that they should also be able to bring modern domestic skills to the household. Women were informed about such things through magazines and manuals published in North Indian languages aimed at teaching women about the management of the modern home – cooking, keeping accounts of domestic expenditure, child-rearing, hygiene and married life. These were all compiled and written by English-educated Indian men although, by the twentieth century, they were being produced by Indian women themselves. One magazine – *Stribodh* (Enlightenment of Women) – first published in 1857, told women that they should use their leisure time to read about domestic matters and self-improvement techniques. There were instructions on sewing, embroidery, advice about how to arrange furniture and how to hire servants. The proper way of using a knife and fork was detailed as well as the moral benefits to be derived from Western practices such as the wearing of shoes and socks. There were also explicit instructions on how the modern woman should provide for her husband on his return from a day at the office.

Agriculture 1860 to 1920

As has been noted, Indian products were now being made available to a global market and Indian peasant farmers had to adapt to the production of such products for export. Commercial export crops such as cotton, jute, wheat, oilseeds, tea, indigo and opium, that could be grown for cash, were cultivated at the expense of local food crops. One problem was that in order to be able to pay the revenue on their land and often to buy seed crops, cash was an absolute necessity for the farmers. That pushed them, very often, into the hands of unscrupulous moneylenders.

This commercialisation of agriculture radically changed rural India and the number of people employed on the land rose by 28 per cent. Farmers were now at the mercy of an ever-fluctuating world market, however, and many amassed debt they had no hope of paying off and many consequently lost their land. An example of how damaging the reliance on global factors could be is shown by the cotton shortage during the 1860s and 1870s as a result of the American Civil War. Indian peasant farmers were exhorted by the Company to cultivate cotton in order to fill the gap. Eventually, however, when the American farmers resumed cultivation and their cotton re-entered the market around the world, the price of Indian cotton plummeted and the rural economy was devastated.

The focus on commercial crops had one dreadful consequence – famine. Indians were, of course, no strangers to famines, having endured them from at least the twelfth century. In other times, however, monsoon rains or crop failure were the causes and a famine was usually limited to just one region. Famines were now more widespread and after one of these events there usually followed epidemics of infectious diseases. There was an outbreak of bubonic plague, for example, that killed around 12.5 million people between 1896 and 1926. Eight hundred thousand died in the 'Orissa Famine' of 1866 and 1867 that spread down the coast through the Madras Presidency and also struck Hyderabad and Mysore. In the next few decades there was a series of famines. Four hundred thousand died in the western Ganges, Rajasthan, central India and the northern Deccan in 1868-70; there was severe famine in Bengal and eastern India in 1873-74; and in the Ganges region as well as the cities of Madras, Hyderabad, Mysore and Bombay people went hungry in 1876-78. There were two severe famines across the entire country. In 1896-97, 96 million Indians were affected and more than 5 million died. In 1899-1900, 60 million were affected and again 5 million died.

The British Indian government was officially in denial about the famines, blaming the monsoon rains and generally unfavourable weather, claiming that intervention by the authorities would only make matters worse. Eventually, however, during the late 1870s, outrage in Britain forced them into action. The Liberal Viceroy, George Robinson, Marquess of Ripon (1827-1909) introduced the Famine Code, a series of regulations that would help the government calculate the severity of a famine and give warning of when intervention was necessary. They also allowed for grain to be moved quickly into regions affected by shortages.

Unrest

The British were never again threatened by a rebellion as serious as that of 1857 but the many pressures of life under British rule – indebtedness, famine and land revenues – resulted in minor uprisings. These were largely regional, tribal, communal or caste rebellions, organised not by regional leaders, chiefs or *zamindars*. The rebellions after 1857 emanated from people of a lower caste or class and the British were not always the target for their anger.

Castes and tribes were often known to the British as the Depressed Classes. They are now categorised in the Indian Constitution as Scheduled Castes and Scheduled Tribes. There are 645 distinct tribes, all linked by kinship rather than class, and they were then often located where cultivated land came up against forests. By the second half of the nineteenth century tribes still constituted around 10 per cent of the total Indian population. They hunted and gathered and paid no revenue for the exploitation of the forests. The British government was keen to force these people into cultivation which would, of course, have resulted in them paying taxes for the land they would be working. This led to violent confrontations from the 1850s until the 1920s, involving the Santhals of northeast India in 1855, the Naikda in Gujarat in 1868 and various tribes in the Madras Presidency from 1879 to 1900. The most significant rebellion was that of the Munda tribespeople of southern Bihar between 1899 and 1900. Their lands had been taken from them by Hindu migrants and the British government. They were led by share-cropper Birsa Munda (1875-1900), a man with some missionary education who would become an inspiration to the later Indian independence movement. He claimed to be a messenger of God, a new prophet, and urged his followers to kill Hindus, Christians and Muslims. His people attacked churches and police stations before many were captured and jailed, including Birsa who died in prison. On the Malabar Coast a series of violent confrontations occurred between the Moplahs, a Muslim community, and their upper-caste Hindu landlords who had been given landlord rights by the British.

The disgruntled Moplahs rose up in 1836, 1854, 1882 to 1885, 1896 and 1921. Meanwhile, in the Deccan and eastern India, peasants, burdened with debt and high land revenues, rioted in 1875 after cotton prices had fallen following the re-entry of the Americans into the cotton market after the American Civil War. A terrible famine ensued and many peasants became bandits in order to survive. Peasant movements organised in eastern Bengal, Assam and Bombay, protesting against land revenues and rent increases. Later, 'no revenue' movements appeared in Surat and Ahmadabad.

Following the Second Afghan War of 1878 to 1880, the government attempted to prevent criticism of the expense of the war with the Vernacular Press Act of 1878. This required Indian-language presses to post bonds with the government guaranteeing their conduct. There was outrage from the owners of the presses and Indian readers and new political associations began to spring up to protest and demand the repeal of the act.

The political associations, run by English-educated Indians, focused their attention on the actions and policies of the British Indian government, using the language and concepts of British constitutional democracy. They petitioned regional governments on issues that were important to people like themselves – middle-class communities – and were particularly interested in issues such as the civil service examinations, further involvement of Indians in the government's Legislative Councils and the cost of the Afghan War and famine relief.

Chapter Ten

Fighting for Freedom

The Educated Elite

The Indian nationalist movement was started by the men of the English-educated elite who sought ways to break through into the imperially controlled government of India. They began to speak of protecting Indian culture and religion and dreamed of independence and *swaraj* – self-rule.

The issues for this educated elite were, as we have seen, representation on Legislative Councils and access to positions with the Indian Civil Service. They were also concerned about the harm done by Indian wealth that was sent to Britain without any benefit to Indians. There were problems about how to approach it, however. Should they be freedom fighters? Social reformers? Hindu revivalists? Or, perhaps, an opposition party? Unfortunately, these questions took up a lot of the nationalists' time and energy and there was a great deal of infighting amongst the various factions.

The British authorities had, of course, begun to sense the feelings of disquiet and between 1885 and 1920 they made a number of concessions to the growing mood of the country, allowing some participation in government. In reality, however, little power was conceded to Indians. Behind the scenes, they played one faction against the other, curating rivalries between, for instance, Muslims and Hindus or Untouchables and Brahmins. Ultimately, it was British actions – especially those of 1905 and 1919 – that brought the disparate elements of Indian nationalism together.

The Indian National Congress

The Indian National Congress was founded in 1885 by Indian and British members of the Theosophical Society movement. The idea is said to have been conceived by 17 men who assembled after a Theosophical Convention held in Madras in December 1874. The first Indian National Union meeting was convened a year later, its objectives to gain participation for Indians in government and to create a platform for political and civic dialogue between educated Indians and the British Indian government. The civil service examinations were also very important to them as they offered the only governmental power that Indians could access. The examinations were open but were held only in England and 19 was the maximum age for those sitting the exam. Thus, in 1880, the 900 employees of the Indian Civil Service featured just 16 Indians. The National Congress met each December, its delegates representing every Indian province. Fifty-four were Hindus, two were Muslim and the remainder were from the Jain or Parsi communities. The organisation's secretary was Allan Octavian Hume (1829-1912), a retired member of the Indian Civil Service who believed that such meetings would allow the educated elite to vent some steam and calm them down. Some of the delegates had already met, and had been associated with the Parsi intellectual, Dadabhai Naoroji (1825-1917) in England in the 1860s and 1870s. Others had met while protesting against the Vernacular Press Act. The Congress was very limited in its first years. Hume was its only full-time officer but it grew rapidly, expanding from 73 delegates in 1885 to almost 2,000 in 1889, 14 per cent of them Muslim.

In 1892, the maximum age for the civil service exam was finally raised to 23 and that same year, the Indian Councils Act allowed for indirect elections to be held for places on the regional Legislative Councils in Bombay, Bengal and Madras. It was a complicated procedure but it did bring some well-known local leaders to the fore. Nonetheless, the civil service examinations would continue to be staged in England until the 1920s.

Hindu and Muslim Disquiet

There were numerous riots, Hindu against Muslim, across the north of the subcontinent in the 1880s and 1890s. These were over the issue of the Muslim slaughter of cows for meat. Cows are, of course, sacred to Hindus and they felt as if their religious practices and way of life were not being adequately protected. The Punjab erupted in 1883 and, from 1888 to 1893, there was trouble between the members of the two religions in the United Provinces, Bihar and Bengal. Bombay saw violent fighting between 1893 and 1895.

Cow protection societies, funded by local elites, sprang up among the Hindus of northern India, and they petitioned the government to prohibit the Muslim slaughter of cows on the grounds of hygiene. The situation was made worse by competition between members of the Hindu and Muslim elites for government jobs, and the violence escalated. By the late nineteenth century the two communities that had once participated in each other's religious festivals were completely split, heightening tensions in the subcontinent.

Hindus were angered even more when the controversial 1891 Age of Consent Act raised the age of consent for sexual intercourse for girls from 10 to 12 years of age. The Indian National Congress supported the act for which many reformers had long been agitating but opposition in Bengal and western India was strong. *Bangabasi*, a conservative Bengali newspaper, declared: 'The Hindu family is ruined.' Mass meetings and demonstrations were held, sometimes erupting into violence. Nonetheless, the bill became law and reformers were vilified in parts of the country. Congress was determined not to let such reforms end their struggle. One of its founders, Surendranath Banerjee (1848-1925) said that it would include in its membership 'those who would reform their social customs and those who would not.'

The Partition of Bengal

In 1905, the British Indian government partitioned Bengal, providing Indians with a reason to unite in defiance of the authorities and stage a national protest. The partition would bring many into the nationalist fold. The decision to partition the province was planned during the term of office of the Viceroy, the autocratic and imperious George Curzon, 1st Marquess Curzon (1859-1925). Bengal was India's largest province, with 78.5 million inhabitants in 1901, making it difficult to govern. The aim was to combine the largely Muslim eastern part of Bengal with Assam while the predominantly Hindu western section was merged with Bihar and Orissa. For the British, the benefit was that Muslims were given a separate province in which they were the majority. Critically, it also made the Hindus a minority in both provinces. According to a government memo this allowed the government 'to split up and thereby weaken a solid body of opponents to our rule'. Hindus were, naturally, outraged at what they rightly saw as a policy of 'divide and rule'.

The British were surprised by the scale of the protests that were led by three radicals – Lala Lajpat Rai (1865-1928), from the Punjab, Bal Gangadhar Tilak (1856-1920), from Pune, and Bipin Chandra Pal (1858-1932), from Bengal, fondly known as 'Lal', 'Bal' and 'Pal'. There were mass meetings and marches and protests persisted for several years, spreading to Bombay, Madras and the Punjab, the protesters included large numbers of English-educated students and professionals. Initially Congress threw its weight behind them but, as the demonstrations became increasingly violent, they withdrew support. Leaders issued instructions for a boycott of British goods and for people to purchase *swadeshi*, Indian-produced products. By 1906, there were noticeable reductions in imported products. Cotton fabrics were down 22 per cent, cotton threads 44 per cent, cigarettes 55 per cent and imported footwear had fallen by 68 per cent. By 1908, imports were generally down by a quarter. The *swadeshi* movement would become a leitmotif of Indian independence efforts.

Shops and schools shut down and imported goods were burned in huge bonfires. The song of the movement – 'Bande Mataram' (Bow to the Mother) – was on everyone's lips:

'Bow to the Mother!
Watered by swiftly flowing rivers,
Rich with abundant fruits, Cooled by lovely southern breezes,
Dark with harvest crops, the Mother…
When 70 million voices roar out your call,
And twice 70 million hands hold sharp, unwavering swords,
Why, Mother, do they call you weak?'

Acts of terrorism were committed, bombs exploded and there were assassination attempts on a number of senior British officials. Middle-class students were arrested, leaders of the protests were incarcerated and public meetings were banned. The new Liberal government at Westminster, realising something would have to be done to end the protests, began to consider constitutional reform. Meanwhile, the government in India tried to quash the *swadeshi* movement. Colleges that supported the campaign were threatened with having their funding withdrawn and *swadeshi* committees were banned. Lajpat Rai was deported to Mandalay in Burma without trial in 1907. Tilak was arrested in 1908 and charged with sedition and sixteen people died during the protests and general strike that ensued after he had been sentenced to six years' imprisonment.

The Muslim League

Muslim involvement in the Indian National Congress was a thorny issue in the late nineteenth and early twentieth centuries. The Muslim leader Sir Syed Ahmad Khan argued that Hindus and Muslims were two disparate communities. He encouraged the Muslim community to be independent of the Hindus and he was not convinced that India's various peoples could ever come together for the sake of national unity. Increasingly, with cow protection protests by Hindus and communal conflict across northern India, Indian Muslims became unwilling to participate in the Indian National Congress, and Muslim membership fell from a high of 14 per cent in 1887 to around 7 per cent between 1893 and 1905. The partition of Bengal pushed Muslims further away from Congress as it proved beneficial to Muslims.

In 1906, 35 prominent Muslims, mostly from wealthy families from the United Provinces, held a meeting at Simla with the Viceroy, Gilbert Elliot-Murray-Kynynmound, Earl of Minto (1845-1914) whose grandfather had been Governor-General of India from 1807 to 1813. At the forefront of the Muslims was Aga Khan III (1877-1957), spiritual leader of the Nizari Ismaili Muslims and a very wealthy man. The aim was for the Muslims to tell Minto that they must be treated as a distinct electorate within India, the only way, they believed, for them to gain a voice amongst elected representatives. The Hindus were in the majority and, as things stood, only Hindus would get elected. Of course, this fitted in perfectly with the British policy of 'divide and rule' and Minto assured them that Muslim interests would be taken into account in any constitutional reforms. It is worth noting that at this point they were not seeking a separate Muslim state.

Shortly afterwards, the All-India Muslim League was founded at Dacca. It allowed only Muslim members and its aim was to protect Muslim rights and liberties, keeping the Muslim community informed of the actions of the British Indian government, discouraging violence and promoting understanding between Muslims and all other Indians. Indian Muslims now had their own political grouping to match the Hindus' Indian National Congress.

Constitutional Reform

In 1909, what came to be known as the Morley-Minto Reforms were announced in the Indian Councils Act. These gave Indians the right to be elected to Legislative Councils, although British representatives still held the majority of places. The means of selection was 'direct elections' from specific constituencies – municipalities, district boards, landowning groups, universities and others. In the act, the British also conceded somewhat to

Muslims' demands for a separate electorate; only Muslims could vote for candidates standing for the Muslim seats and there were six within the landlord constituencies of the Imperial Legislative Council and others in the provincial councils. Secretary of State for India, John Morley (1838-1923) denied that such reforms would inevitably lead to independence for India: 'If it could be said that this chapter of reforms led directly or indirectly to the establishment of a parliamentary system in India, I for one would have nothing at all to do with it.' Indeed, the Morley-Minto Reforms were insufficient for more radical Indian nationalists, although the more moderate who were interested in elections and appointments were happy with them.

The concessions of the Morley-Minto Reforms were a source of anger and conflict right up until independence in 1947. As more Indians were brought into government in years to come, Muslims fought hard to retain or even to increase the number of seats reserved for them while Hindus strived to eliminate them, considering them undemocratic and a hindrance in the creation of a national Indian ethos shared by Hindu and Muslim alike.

A much greater concession was made two years later at a great durbar that was held in Delhi, celebrating the accession of King George V. The British revoked the 1905 partition of Bengal and a new partition was introduced that divided the province on a linguistic rather than a religious basis. Bengali-speaking Indians were reunited in a smaller new province to be called Bengal while Bihar and Orissa became a separate province and Assam Province was created to the east. At the same time, the Viceroy punished the Bengalis, by moving the capital from Calcutta closer to the summer capital of Simla and further away from the troubles of Bengal. Architects Sir Edwin Lutyens (1869-1944) and Sir Herbert Baker (1862-

1946) were engaged to re-design the British section of Delhi and the British Indian government would have its capital in New Delhi.

The re-unification of Bengal pleased neither nationalists nor Muslims and the bitterness persisted until the opening of the new capital in 1912 when a bomb went off, almost killing the Viceroy, Charles Hardinge (1858-1948), grandson of former Governor-General, Henry Hardinge. There were further terrorist acts in the Punjab. Meanwhile, the Muslim League changed its position, embracing the goal of self-government.

The First World War

Great Britain's declaration of war with Germany on 4 August, 1914 also meant, of course, that its empire, including India, was at war with Germany and her allies. Most Indian nationalists came together to support Britain in this time of grave crisis, but they were hoping as they did so that their support would lead to further steps towards self-government. Even Tilak, who was released from prison that year encouraged his fellow Hindus to sign up and fight for the Empire. 1.4 million Indian and British soldiers of the British Indian Army fought in the European, Mediterranean and Middle East theatres during the conflict. Nearly 62,000 lost their lives in the fighting and 67,000 were wounded.

Meanwhile, at home, India's export business suffered from losing Germany and Austria-Hungary as customers. Pre-war, they had represented the country's second-largest market. Income taxes, import duties and prices all went up, prices by more than 50 per cent between 1914 and 1918. There were food shortages as a result of the huge amount of wheat that was being exported to Britain and its allies. This was not helped by a poor monsoon and an influenza outbreak that killed 12 million people. Things were so bad that the Indian government passed laws helping large landowners but poorer farmers received little aid. Protests and strikes were held against landlords throughout the Ganges valley. Congress did not participate, anxious not to antagonise the landlords who were one of the important constituencies in elections. Nonetheless, industries such as iron, steel and cotton prospered as they filled the gaps left by European suppliers caught up in the conflict. After the war, India emerged as the fourth largest industrial power in the world.

There was a great deal of industrial action in the early 1920s and Congress founded the All-India Trade Union in 1920. That same year, Manabendra Nath Roy (1887-1954) founded the Communist Party of India which began organising strikes in the jute, cloth and steel industries. In the first six months of 1920 there were more than 200 strikes and, by the end of the decade, almost a quarter of a million workers were trade union members.

The Changing of the Nationalist Guard

In preparation for the end of the war and possible concessions from the British government, Indian nationalist leaders looked for ways to keep the movement alive when the world's eyes were focused elsewhere. In 1916, Tilak founded a 'home rule league' in Pune and Annie Besant (1847-1933), the British socialist and theosophist and staunch supporter of Indian self-determination, did likewise in Madras. Soon, there were chapters across the country and around 30,000 members. That same year, the Indian National Congress and the Muslim League buried the hatchet at Lucknow in the Lucknow Pact. They had been brought together by Muhammad Ali Jinnah (1876-1948), leader of the All-India Muslim League, as it was now called, as well as a member of Congress. They resolved to work together for greater power for Indians and also accepted the principle of separate constituencies for Muslims. They demanded that 50 per cent of the places on the Executive Council should be occupied by Indians.

This unlikely pact came about largely because of the passing of older nationalist leaders. Indeed, two younger men emerged who would have a large part to play in the future of the subcontinent – Muhammad Ali Jinnah and Mohandas K Gandhi (1869-1948).

Muhammad Ali Jinnah

Born and educated in Karachi, Muhammad Ali Jinnah was the son of a middle-class Muslim merchant of the Khoja people. His father's family were Gujarati and had migrated to Sind. Jinnah was sent to England in 1892, where he studied law at Lincoln's Inn and was influenced by nineteenth-century British liberalism, as were many other future Indian independence leaders. He became involved in Indian nationalist politics while working on the parliamentary campaign of Dadabhai Naoroji, the first Asian Member of Parliament in Britain.

Returning to India, Jinnah established a successful law practice in Bombay. He was a delegate to the 1906 Congress and was elected, following the Morley-Minto Reforms, to the Imperial Legislative Council in 1910. He impressed everyone, Indian and British alike, with his debonair appearance, his skilful arguments and his English habits.

He joined the All-India Muslim League in 1913 after it declared that its goal was now self-government. His vision was of the League and Congress working in a united fashion to provide opposition to British rule in India and, ultimately, to achieve independence.

Mohandas K Gandhi

Mohandas Karamchand Gandhi (1869-1948) was also born in Gujarat, into a Hindu merchant caste family, his father serving at one point as *diwan* (chief minister) in their home state of Porbandar. Gandhi was educated in India before travelling in 1887 to London to study law at the Inner Temple. Returning in 1890 to India, he found it difficult to make a success of his career in Gujarat or Bombay. Therefore, in 1893 he travelled to South Africa where he lived and worked for 22 years. It was there that he discovered his vocation as a political organiser as well as his Hindu faith. He worked for the resident Indian community's rights.

Indians in South Africa were of all religious persuasions and came from across the subcontinent. Gandhi believed that their 'Indianness' could transcend religion and caste and led them in a variety of protests against British laws which discriminated against Indians. He himself experienced discrimination and even beatings for his nationality. He fought to obtain the vote for Indians and founded the Natal Indian Congress in 1894. From 1907 to 1911, he led non-violent campaigns and was arrested in 1913 when he led several thousand people in a 'Great March' across the country.

While in South Africa, Gandhi developed the non-violent resistance tactic of *satyagraha* (literally 'holding firmly to truth'), something he would later use to dramatic effect in India. Basically, it was about peacefully refusing to obey discriminatory or unfair legislation. He later recalled:

'[I had] to choose between allying myself to violence or finding out some other method of stopping the rot, and it came to me that we should refuse to obey legislation that was degrading and let them put us in jail if they liked.'

By the time he returned to India in 1915, he was already famous, and he had gained a great deal of political experience and knowledge that would prove useful in the years to come. He had also found a way to bring together the Western education of his youth and his Hindu faith. By this time he was wearing a simple Indian costume – a *dhoti*, which is a long cloth wrapped around the lower body, a shawl and a turban. He believed in the principle that the means by which a political goal was achieved was just as important as the eventual result. He began to undertake long and perilous fasts that were intended to convince his opponents of the truth of what he was saying. The British, of course, viewed him as suspicious.

The Amritsar Massacre

Having supported Britain wholeheartedly during the war, Indian nationalists had every right to expect some form of reward at its conclusion. The reforms, when they came, however, disappointed nationalists, no matter which faction they belonged to. The Montagu-Chelmsford (popularly known as the Mont-Ford) Reforms were devised by Samuel Montagu (1879-1924), Liberal Secretary of State for India, and Frederic Thesiger, Lord Chelmsford (1868-1933), Viceroy of India. They appeared in the Government of India Act 1919 and offered Indians dual government at the provincial level. The act also transferred control of a number of government departments, including education, public health and agriculture, to Indian ministers who would be elected. Other departments such as justice, land revenue and the police remained with the British.

The nationalists were dismayed that Indians were only going to be given control over traditionally underfunded departments and would have no say in the way government was funded. Congress was divided, moderates considering setting up a separate party that would accept the Mont-Ford Reforms. Soon, however, there was an issue on which all nationalists could agree. During the war the Defence of India Act had been introduced that had allowed for certain political cases to be tried without a jury. In 1918, the British Indian government passed the Rowlatt Act which made the measures of the Defence of India Act permanent. There was immediate outrage. Jinnah resigned his seat on the Legislative Council and Gandhi called for a national strike. When the strike became violent, however, Gandhi announced its end. In Amritsar, the government responded aggressively to the protests, banning public meetings. Undeterred, on 13 April 1919, around 5,000 people gathered at Jallianwalla Bagh (Jallianwalla Garden) to celebrate the annual religious festival of Baisakhi. Brigadier-General Reginald Dyer, commander-in-charge of Amritsar, ordered 50 of his troops to block the entrance to the garden before ordering them to open fire on the unarmed protesters as they tried to leave the garden. They killed what the British estimated to be 379 but the Indians reckoned to be as many as 1,500. Gandhi described the British report on the massacre as 'page after page of thinly disguised official whitewash'. Dyer was forced in the end to resign from the army and the Indian Hunter Commission condemned him for his action that day but in Great Britain he was celebrated as a hero, especially amongst those who had connections with the British Raj.

In India, naturally, there was horror and outrage. Indians

were united in their anger and in their vehement opposition to the British. Rabindranath Tagore had received a knighthood in 1913 after winning the Nobel Prize for Literature but he was so dismayed by the Amritsar Massacre that he returned it. In 1919, Congress symbolically moved its annual assembly to Amritsar where it was attended by 38,000 people. Gandhi would use these events to take Congress out into the villages of India. He now led a mass movement for self-government in the subcontinent.

Chapter Eleven

Towards Independence:
The Nationalist Movement from
1920 to 1948

Non-Cooperation

The Khilafat Movement was a pan-Islamic, protest organisation campaigning against the British government to maintain the Ottoman sultan's role as caliph – leader of Muslims worldwide – after the war. It was led by two brothers, Muhammad (1878-1931), who was a graduate of Oxford University, and Shaukat Ali (1873-1938) who launched an Indian branch of Khilafat in June 1920 at an event attended by Gandhi and several other nationalist leaders. The leaders of the group announced a programme of non-cooperation with the British India government and Gandhi gave it the support of his Home Rule League. It began without the official sanction of Congress, but at a hastily arranged emergency conference, members supported it, to the annoyance of leaders such as Jinnah who, having argued for constitutional and moderate protest, resigned.

In 1921, therefore, Gandhi assumed leadership of the Indian National Congress and that year launched the campaign of non-cooperation. He expanded his programme to include the *swadeshi* tactic of boycotting British goods, further advocating the boycotting of British schools, colleges and courts. He invited Indians to resign from their jobs with the government and to decline British titles and honours. He also advocated that *khadi* (homespun goods) be worn, instead of the British-made textiles that were increasingly common. He encouraged men and women to take a little time each day to spin *khadi* in a show of support for the movement for independence and even invented a small portable spinning wheel. It was a clever tactic to imbue his followers with discipline, but also to make women feel part of the movement.

Non-cooperation was widely practised and Gandhi and Khilafat brought India very close to all-out rebellion. By December 1921, 30,000 Indians had been sent to prison for civil disobedience and all public meetings had been banned. The Ali brothers were under arrest, as were most of the leaders of Congress.

In the midst of this upheaval, the Muslim leaders of Khilafat began to consider abandoning non-violence and, indeed, violence had already broken out. In February 1922 in Chauri Chaura, Uttar Pradesh, 22 police officers died in a fire in their police station started by protesters. On hearing of this, Gandhi immediately announced the end of the campaign. He was arrested the following month for sedition and sentenced to six years' imprisonment. He proudly told the court:

'I am here… to invite and cheerfully submit to the highest penalty that can be inflicted upon me… I hold it an honour to be disaffected towards a government which in its totality has done India more harm than any previous system.'

He served two years before his release in 1924 but, during his incarceration, Congress had begun to split. One faction, led by

Chitta Ranjan Das (1869-1925) and Motilal Nehru (1861-1931) – founder of the Nehru/Gandhi political dynasty – favoured participation in the legislatures; the other, led by Chakravarti Rajagopalachari (1878-1972) and Sardar Vallabhbhai Patel (1875-1950) opposed it. Gandhi's efforts to bridge the gap between opposing factions and between Muslims and Hindus climaxed in a three-week fast in 1924 but this was not entirely successful. He rejected the opportunity to embark on further anti-British campaigns, focusing instead on relief projects and work in villages. He would not re-enter the political arena until 1929.

More reforms were announced in the 1921 India Act, and the Legislative Council became a bicameral parliament with elected members. There were the first moves to introduce Indian fiscal control with a new Tariff Board in New Delhi and the civil service exams were, for the first time, held simultaneously in India as well as England.

In the municipal elections of 1923-24 Congress did well, winning mayoral elections in a number of towns and cities. But separate electorates again caused conflict between Hindu and Muslim. There were numerous communal riots in the 1920s and the days of Hindu-Muslim political unity were well and truly over.

The Simon Commission

The British government set up a commission, headed by a politician, Sir John Simon (1873-1954), to tour India, investigating what further political reforms were needed. It immediately caused trouble because it did not include any Indians, leading to protests and demonstrations wherever its members turned up. Congress, the Muslim League and most other Indian political groups refused to have anything to do with it.

In 1928, the nationalists held an All-Parties Conference with the objective of developing a separate Indian plan for reform as a counter to anything proposed by the Simon Commission. They resolved that the objective of Indian nationalism should be a self-governing India with Commonwealth status within the British Empire. It could not be agreed, however, how minorities would be represented in the ensuing government.

The Simon Commission recommended the establishment of representative government in the provinces and that separate communal electorates be retained, but only until the tensions between Hindus and Muslims had calmed. In September 1928, prior to the Commission's release of its report, Motilal Nehru presented his 'Nehru Report' in which he argued against charges that Indians could not find a constitutional consensus among themselves. He recommended that India be given Dominion status and complete internal self-government.

As a result of the Simon Commission, the Government of India Act 1935 established representative government at the provincial level in India. The first elections held in the provinces in 1937 would result in the return of Congress governments almost everywhere.

In 1929, Gandhi gave in to pleas to re-enter political life. He arranged for Jawaharlal Nehru to be elected President of Congress and, with Nehru at the helm, the party abandoned the notion of Commonwealth status, advocating instead complete independence. Gandhi, it was decided, would spearhead a new civil disobedience campaign the following year.

Muslims would not be standing beside their Hindu countrymen. Muhammad Ali Jinnah, dissatisfied with Congress, had transferred his allegiance to the All-India Muslim League that was meeting in New Delhi and which announced its support for separate constituencies. Muslims and Hindu politicians were once again at loggerheads, Jinnah accusing Gandhi of supporting Mahasabha, a north Indian Hindu political grouping founded in 1915 by Madan Mohan Malaviya (1861-1946). It had formed Hindu self-defence corps, had demanded the replacement of Urdu by Hindi and made efforts to convert Muslims and Untouchables to the Hindu faith. By 1925, it had a paramilitary wing.

The Great Depression and India

The Wall Street Crash and the ensuing financial chaos had a huge, detrimental impact on India's economy as well as on its economic relationship with Britain. Britain was very important to Indian businesses, and 11 per cent of all goods imported into Britain before 1929 originated in the subcontinent. Indian imports made a huge contribution to the favourable balance of trade that Britain enjoyed in world markets but the Depression changed this. The value of Indian exports was cut by more than 50 per cent and Indian imports fell by about the same amount. In India, agricultural prices plummeted between 1929 and 1931 which impacted upon tax payments by peasant landlords. The British Indian government was forced to dip into its gold reserves and it was no longer as profitable for British companies to invest directly in India. They chose, instead, to develop partnerships with Indian companies. At the same time, there was a growth in Indian industry across the country, textile mills, for instance, supplying about two-thirds of all textiles purchased in India by the 1930s. Some of the money earned by the captains of Indian industry found its way into a grateful Congress's coffers.

Nonetheless, India was marked by poverty and stagnation in

the 1930s as agriculture declined and she was forced to import food. Food production was failing to support the growing population of 389 million.

The Salt March

At midnight on 31 December 1929, members of the Indian National Congress raised the flag of India on the banks of the Ravi River at Lahore. They had publicly issued the *Purna Swaraj* or declaration of sovereignty and self-rule. The statement said:

'We believe that it is the inalienable right of the Indian people, as of any other people, to have freedom and to enjoy the fruits of their toil and have the necessities of life, so that they may have full opportunities of growth. We believe also that if any government deprives a people of these rights and oppresses them the people have a further right to alter it or abolish it. The British government in India has not only deprived the Indian people of their freedom but has based itself on the exploitation of the masses, and has ruined India economically, politically, culturally and spiritually. We believe therefore, that India must sever the British connection and attain *Purna Swaraj* or complete sovereignty and self-rule.'

They requested that the people of India observe 26 January as Independence Day and across India that day the Indian tricolour was hoisted by Congress members, nationalists and the general public.

Everyone was surprised by Gandhi's choice of the salt tax as the focus of his campaign. The British had made it illegal for Indians to make their own salt, even to pick it up on the beach or reclaim it from the sea without paying the tax on it. It was a tax that affected every Indian, the poor disproportionately more than the wealthy, of course. Typically, for one of Gandhi's campaigns, it was an issue with political as well as ethical dimensions.

On 12 March, Gandhi and 70 others departed from his ashram at Sabarmati. By 6 April, 24 days later, they had walked 240 miles to Dandi on the coast of Gujarat where they made salt without tendering any tax, Gandhi breaking the salt laws at 6.30 that morning. He urged Indians all over the country also to break the salt laws and to boycott British goods:

'It is a non-violent struggle… If you feel strong enough, give up Government jobs, enlist yourselves as soldiers in this salt *satyagraha*, burn your foreign cloth and wear *khadi*. Give up liquor. There are many things within your power through which you can secure the keys which will open the gates of freedom.'

His protest brought global attention on India and civil disobedience broke out across the country. Congress illegally sold salt in Ahmadabad and 10,000 people bought it. This was repeated in Bombay. Jawaharlal Nehru was arrested on 14 April and Gandhi on 4 May but the protests continued. Although they sometimes turned violent, on this occasion Gandhi did not call a halt to the campaign.

It was a far greater show of discontent than ever, demonstrating the growing influence of Congress but the police reaction, even to peaceful protesters, was ruthless and more than 60,000 people were jailed, around twice as many as during the last protest.

The Poona Pact and the Government of India Act 1935

A couple of Round Table Conferences on the future of government in India came up with no agreement between the various parties which led to the British deciding unilaterally on the award of separate electorates to Muslims, Sikhs, Indian Christians, Europeans, women and the Untouchables. Gandhi believed the Untouchables to be Hindus and that as such they should not be separated from the Hindu vote. He began a fast, and the British moved swiftly to get a new agreement in place before he died. On 24 September, they signed the Poona Pact which gave a separate electoral position to the Untouchables. Gandhi ended his fast but began touring Untouchable communities, creating recruits for Congress.

The Government of India Act 1935 was seen by some as a back-door route to giving India Dominion status while others viewed it as an attempt to remove some of the power of Congress in India. It purportedly gave a large measure of autonomy to India and made provision for a Federation of India that would be made up of British India and some or all of the Princely States. This never happened due to opposition from the heads of the Princely States and Congress also opposed it. Direct elections were introduced, however, raising the electorate from 7 million to 35 million. More elected Indian representatives were to be allowed on provincial assemblies although the provincial Governors retained special powers and could suspend a government.

As has been noted, in the provincial elections of 1937, Congress's power base was emphasised by a sweeping victory, winning 70 per cent of the popular vote and 8 of the 11 provinces. The Muslim League won only 5 per cent of the total Muslim vote and control of none of the Muslim provinces, which were won by regional parties and, in one case, Congress.

Jinnah Proposes Pakistan

Jinnah's Muslim League had been devastated by the 1937 elections, leaving him with the unenviable task of trying to re-build his party. He did so in the 1940s with the notion of a separate autonomous state for India's Muslims. He had reached the conclusion that there was no constitutional approach to India that would benefit the Muslim community. The League's 1940 Lahore Resolution stated that:

'...the areas in which the Muslims are generally in a majority... should be grouped to constitute "Independent States" in which the constituent units shall be autonomous and sovereign.'

The idea was not new. Sir Syed Ahmad Khan had championed the two-nation theory and, in his presidential address to the Muslim League in 1930, Allama Iqbal (1877-1938) had called for 'the amalgamation of North-West Muslim-majority Indian states'. A name – 'Pakistan' – had even been coined for it in 1933 by Choudhry Rahmat Ali (1895-1951), a Muslim student at Cambridge University. The word meant 'pure land' but it was also an acronym representing the names of the main regions of the Muslim north – 'P' for the Punjab; 'A' for Afghanistan; 'K' for Kashmir; 'S' for Sind and 'tan' for Baluchistan.

Some have alleged that Jinnah's promotion of Pakistan began as a means to popularise the Muslim League after the disasters of 1937 or a threat to force concessions from Congress. He may have believed this might work especially with Gandhi who was horrified by the thought of India splitting up. The problem for the Muslim League was that Indian Muslims were not concentrated in a few provinces. They were scattered throughout the subcontinent. Nonetheless, the idea still appealed greatly to many Muslims.

The Quit India Movement

On 1 September, 1939, Germany invaded Poland and two days later, Britain declared war. That day, the Viceroy, Victor Hope, 2nd Marquess Linlithgow (1887-1952) announced, on the orders of Westminster, that India, too, was at war with Germany. Congress offered its support conditionally, demanding that it be given a share in India's government. Winston Churchill, British prime minister after May 1940, was adamant that no concessions be given although a promise of Dominion status was offered, an offer that Gandhi described as little more than a 'post-dated cheque'.

In 1942, a new campaign of civil disobedience named 'Quit India!' was launched, calling for what Gandhi described as 'An Orderly British Withdrawal' from India. He gave a speech outlining the initiative to the All-India Congress Committee and within a few hours the entire leadership of Congress was under arrest. There was a huge response and, by the end of 1943, around 90,000 people had been arrested. Many stayed away from work and some of the protests turned violent. Government buildings were set on fire, bombs were set off, electricity was cut and transport was in chaos. The British response was harsh with police shootings, public floggings and the destruction of villages. There were even aerial machine gun attacks on protesters in eastern Bengal.

While all this was occurring, Bengal suffered another terrible famine that lasted until 1946. For once, the weather could not be blamed. A great deal of food for local consumption had been commandeered by the British army. The supply of rice from Burma was stopped because of the war which made rice unaffordable for many and millions died as a result.

Independence

More than two and a half million Indian soldiers fought in the Second World War and several of the Princely States made large donations to support the Allied effort. India also provided a base for American operations in support of China in the China-Burma-India theatre of the war. Casualties were high and in the first two months of the conflict, 7,000 Indian soldiers lost their lives. By the end of the war, more than 87,000 Indian soldiers had died in the fighting. They fought across the world, in the European theatre against the Germans, in North Africa where they faced the Italians and the Germans, and in the South Asia theatre where they fought the Japanese. They also faced the Japanese in Burma.

By the end of the war, Britain, like much of Europe, faced a massive task of re-building and was burdened with huge debts. India had more than repaid its debt to Britain with supplies and men and Britain was, in reality, in debt to India. In such circumstances, the empire in India was no longer really viable. Withdrawal, however, would not be easy because of the various factions that would somehow have to be accommodated – Muslims, Hindus, Sikhs, South Indian Dravidians and Untouchables, for instance. The task was to put together all these diverse interests in a modern democratic state whilst protecting each of their interests.

In the elections of 1945-46 in India, Congress swept the board, winning 91 per cent of all the non-Muslim seats. They took control in eight provinces, their aim a centralised Indian state. Minority groupings worried that their interests would be ignored in such an entity but for Congress such matters could wait until after the country had won independence. Jinnah's Muslim League did not have the consensus amongst Muslims that Congress enjoyed with India's Hindus. It performed well in the elections, though, winning every Muslim seat at the centre and 439 of the 494 Muslim provincial seats. Muslims sought protection for their religious identity – now a critical part of their political identity before the delivery of independence. Various plans were proposed and rejected leading to Hindu-Muslim rioting across the north in which 4,000 died. The riots spread and in the United Provinces Hindus massacred around 8,000 Muslims.

The British were now in a hurry and new Labour prime minister, Clement Atlee (1883-1967), announced that Britain would be out of India by June 1948. However, when the last Viceroy, Lord Louis Mountbatten (1900-79), arrived in the subcontinent in March 1947, it was announced that the British would make their exit a little earlier – in August of that year. This made it incumbent upon them to come up with a strategy for India's future. They settled for a plan that would create two states with Dominion status – India and Pakistan. Pakistan would be made up of a partitioned Bengal and Punjab, the Northwest Frontier province and Sind. The plan was agreed by all parties – Congress, the Muslim League and the Sikhs on 2 June 1947, the Indian Independence Act was passed at Westminster on 18 July and the date for the handover of power was set for 15 August. The ceremony took place at Parliament House in New Delhi and India at last became independent at midnight on 14 August 1947. Nehru, who became the independent India's first prime minister, said in his speech that night:

'…and now the time comes when we shall redeem our pledge, not wholly or in full measure, but very substantially. At the stroke of the midnight hour, when the world sleeps, India will awake to life and freedom. A moment comes, which comes but rarely in history, when we step out from the old to the new, when an age ends, and when the soul of a nation, long suppressed, finds utterance.'

Partition of India

The British lawyer, Sir Cyril Radcliffe (1899-1977) was given the onerous task of establishing the borders for the two new countries of India and Pakistan, the aim being to leave as many Hindus and Sikhs as possible in India and as many Muslims as possible in Pakistan. He chaired two boundary commissions that were set up and, on 9 August 1947, he submitted his partition map. The new boundaries were announced on 14 August, the day that Pakistan gained independence and the day before India did so.

Of course, the new borders placed many people on the wrong side of the line and resulted in 14 million people, around 7 million from each side, fleeing across the border as soon as they knew the situation. The minorities who remained were attacked, on each side of the border. Many died, estimates of the number of dead varying from several hundred thousand to as many as a million.

The Princely States, which had largely been very supportive of the British in India, were left to fend for themselves. The

British informed them that they would have to sort out their status with whichever of the two states they found themselves in after partition. By 1947, all of them except Junagadh, Hyderabad and Kashmir had accepted generous allowances in exchange for their states and most of them had handed them over to India.

Bordering both new states, Kashmir became a flashpoint for hostilities between them. In January 1949, the United Nations effected a ceasefire between India and Pakistan and brokered a new border that gave India control of two-thirds of the province and Pakistan the remainder. As part of this deal it was agreed that India would stage a referendum to discover what the people of the region wanted to happen. India, however, has refused to conduct such an exercise, leaving Kashmir a troubled area that has been a source of conflict between the two countries ever since.

Meanwhile, Gandhi had withdrawn from the negotiations for independence, finding it difficult to come to terms with the partition of his beloved country. On the other hand, he could see no way round it. He tried to bring a halt to the escalating violence, travelling to eastern India and then fasting in Calcutta. What was to be the final fast of his life took place in Delhi and it stopped the fighting there. On 27 January he delivered a speech to Delhi's Muslims from a Muslim shrine and three days later, on 30 January 1948, he was assassinated by a Hindu nationalist, Nathuram Godse (1910-49), as he walked to his daily prayer meeting in the garden of Birla House in New Delhi. Gandhi was considered to be pro-Muslim by Godse and the Brahmin group in Pune who had planned the assassination. Predictably, rioting broke out in Pune, Nagpur and Bombay.

Chapter Twelve

The Making of a Nation

A New System

The new nation launched with a caretaker administration headed by Jawaharlal Nehru as prime minister and fellow Congress politician Sardar Patel (1875-1950) as his deputy. Nehru's aim was to create a country that was democratic, secular and, if India's poor were to have improved living conditions, socialist. Patel was of the more conservative wing of Congress and, although he said a great deal less in public than Nehru, he had a lot of control over the party. However, his death in 1950 left Nehru virtually unchallenged.

A constitution was drafted that became law on 26 January 1950, granting Indians all the basic civil liberties. It abolished Untouchability and left intact the separate legal codes for the Hindu and Muslim communities that had existed under British law. Government was to be parliamentary with a Supreme Court based on the template of the United States Supreme Court. The regional state governments would be linked to a central government that would have two houses. The Lok Sabha (People's Assembly) was the lower house and its 550 members would be elected by proportional representation for terms of five years. The upper house – the Rajya Sabha (States' Assembly) – would be elected for six-year terms by the provincial legislative assemblies. The government would be whichever party could form a majority. There would also be a president and vice-president although their roles would be purely ceremonial.

The vote was given to all Indians – male and female – over the age of 21 but, although separate electorates were abolished, there were still reserved seats for Scheduled Castes – Untouchables – and Scheduled Tribes. In the first elections, Congress won an overwhelming majority and formed India's first government with Jawaharlal Nehru as prime minister.

The First Years

Much happened in the first few years as India found its feet as a nation. Language became important in the geographic division of the country and in 1956 India was divided into 14 language-based states. Kerala, for instance, was created for speakers of Malayam and Karnakata for those who spoke Kannada. Intercaste barriers to marriage were removed by the 1949 Hindu Marriage Validation Act and the minimum age for marriage was raised to 18 for men and 15 for women. Furthermore, women were given the right to divorce husbands with more than one wife. In 1956, women were given the same claim as men to paternal property and five years later demanding a dowry was rendered illegal. These laws applied only to the Hindu majority, however, since Muslims were governed by their own legal code. In 1955, it became illegal to discriminate against Untouchables.

Nehru launched the first of three five-year plans, the goal of which was economic stability. The economy had suffered many blows – the war, the famine in Bengal and the cost of independence and partition – that had seriously destabilised it. The plan focused on agriculture, transport, industry and power. By 1956, the Indian economy had recovered and the five-year plan was adjudged a success.

The second (1956-61) and third (1961-66) five-year plans focused on developing industry, and by 1965 India was the seventh most industrially advanced country in the world, enjoying success in the production of steel, electricity, cement and chemical fertilisers.

Border Dispute with China and the Death of Nehru

The Cold War was in full swing in the 1950s but Nehru was reluctant to place India on either the side of the United States or the USSR. Instead, he promoted the idea of 'non-aligned' countries, a coalition, as he saw it, of third world nations seeking peaceful coexistence and mutual territorial respect. He had already signed such a treaty with China in which Tibet was recognised as part of China and each of them acknowledged respect for the other's territorial integrity. There was no mention of the actual frontier between India and China, however, and from 1955 to 1959 Chinese forces strayed into territories that India considered hers.

In autumn 1962, with talks on the border issue stalling, the Chinese launched offensives in Ladakh and across the McMahon Line – a line allegedly marking the border between India and China. The Chinese defeated the Indians in both theatres in which the conflict took place, capturing Rezang La in Chushul in the western theatre and Tawang in the eastern. China ended the war by declaring a ceasefire on 20 August 1962 and also withdrew from the area that was under dispute. Around 1,400 Indian troops died in the fighting and 722 Chinese.

The Indian army had been totally unprepared for the war, leading to the resignation of the Defence Minister and a programme of weaponisation as the country tried to become self-sufficient in armament manufacture. Nehru's daughter Indira Gandhi (1917-84) during her time as prime minister completed this process which contributed to India's comprehensive defeat of Pakistan in 1971.

In May 1964, Jawaharlal Nehru died and hundreds of thousands of Indians attended his cremation on the banks of the Yamuna River. His legacy was muddied by the embarrassment of the Sino-Indian War, by the failure of his non-alignment project, especially after India invaded Goa in 1961, and growing doubt as to whether his five-year plans had benefitted the Indian economy after all. It was unclear who would succeed him as prime minister and at first it was believed his daughter would be the inevitable choice, but she declined the offer.

The job fell to Lal Bahadur Shastri (1904-66), a moderate former follower of Gandhi from the United Provinces. He was in office only until 1966, his tenure blighted by an increasing food crisis. There was also protest in the south of the country at the government's plans to make Hindi the official language of India. Eventually, it was decided that three languages could be used – English, a regional language appropriate to the area and Hindi.

Shastri enjoyed some success, however, in 1965, when Indian forces defeated Pakistani troops in a war over India's refusal to hold a referendum in Kashmir.

Indira Gandhi

Lal Bahadur Shastri died suddenly of a heart attack in January 1966, after just one year and 216 days in office, and the leaders of the Congress party selected Nehru's daughter to be his successor. Indira Gandhi – no relation to the Mahatma – was a 48-year-old widow with two sons who had been her father's personal assistant and hostess when required.

As prime minister, she became well known for her political ruthlessness. She argued with senior Congress leaders and was even expelled from the party in 1969, successfully maintaining her own faction of Congress. By 1971, the party had been weakened by its many factional splits and was entirely dependent on her. She won the election of that year on a policy of eradicating poverty but her greatest achievement after that was the defeat of Pakistan in the war of 1971.

East and West Pakistan were a thousand miles apart and each had different interests in terms of the economy, languages and culture. The West dominated the East both politically and economically despite the East having 60 per cent of the population. In 1970, the party of the East Pakistan leader Sheik Mujibur Rahman (1920-75) – known as Sheik Mujib – won the country's first parliamentary election but the President of Pakistan, Agha Muhammad Yahya Khan (1917-80), refused to let him form a government. Rahman declared independence and West Pakistani troops invaded, their campaign bringing terror and bloodshed, in which students, politicians and intellectuals were massacred. The world looked on, horrified by the atrocities and the plight of refugees. By the end of 1971, 10 million East Pakistanis had fled for their lives across the border into India. Rahman was arrested and imprisoned.

India provided financial and material support to East Pakistan which resulted in West Pakistan declaring war in December 1971, bombing Indian airfields. India immediately invaded East Pakistan and overwhelmed the Pakistan army before declaring a ceasefire. East Pakistan became independent as Bangladesh.

The war was good for Congress and Indira Gandhi. In the 1972 State Assembly elections they won 70 per cent of the seats. Crisis was to follow, however. There were crop failures, economic problems, rising food prices and inflation reached 20 per cent. As wages were frozen, strikes broke out and factories closed. The International Monetary Fund provided Gandhi with a loan but only with stringent conditions attached such as cutting expenditure and curtailing aggressive economic policies. Gandhi's pledge to abolish poverty now rang hollow in the ears of India's poor.

She initiated the Green Revolution to try to alleviate the problem of food shortages, the government sponsoring modern farming equipment, new varieties of seeds and financial incentives to farmers. This brought increased agricultural productivity.

By 1972, Gandhi was using the provision from the 1935 Government of India Act to impose emergency conditions on any state that opposed her. It became increasingly difficult to implement her policies and corruption was rife in the government. Strikes and protests against rising prices and inflation continued, even after India became the world's sixth nuclear power in 1974. The protest movement was led by Jayaprakash Narayan (1902-79), founder of the Indian Socialist Party.

In June 1975, after being found guilty in Uttar Pradesh of corrupt election practices, Gandhi was banned from holding office for six years. She persuaded the president to announce that 'a grave emergency exists whereby the security of India is threatened by internal disturbances', and declared a national emergency on 25 June 1975, jailing opponents and initiating censorship measures that shut down the media. Parliament, which was now made up only of her supporters, erased the charges against her and she postponed forthcoming elections. The Emergency, as it is now called, resulted in a growth in industrial production and a fall in prices. She ended it in January 1977. Political prisoners were released, censorship ended and elections for Parliament were announced.

The Janata coalition, led by Narayan and Morarji Desai (1896-1995) defeated Gandhi and Congress, and she and her son Sanjay (1946-80) lost their seats. Janata went after the Gandhis with an investigation into the Emergency and, when she re-entered Parliament in 1978, she was expelled from the Lok Sabha and jailed for a week. Janata, meanwhile, achieved little, prices rising once more and food supplies diminishing. In 1979, the coalition disintegrated and the government fell.

Indira Gandhi Returns to Power

Gandhi's Congress (I) Party – the 'I' standing, of course, for Indira – returned to power in 1980, but within months Sanjay, Indira's political heir, was dead in a light aircraft crash. She replaced him with her other son, Rajiv (1944-91) who was an airline pilot, married to an Italian-born woman, Sonia (b. 1946).

Gandhi began to adopt strategies in the regions that would help her, no matter what they were. In the Punjab the main opponent of Congress was the fairly moderate Sikh party, the Akali Dal, which supported the notion of the Punjab becoming an autonomous Sikh state – Khalistan. To counter Akali Dal, Sanjay Gandhi had championed a militant Sikh holy man named Jarnail Singh Bhindranwale (1947-84). Bhindranwale and his supporters launched a terrorist campaign that was aimed at forcing non-Sikhs to leave the Punjab. Following the shooting of Gurbachan Singh (1930-80), leader of the Sikh reform movement, the Nirankaris, Bhindranwale and others barricaded themselves in July 1983 in the Golden Temple at Amritsar, the Sikh religion's holiest site, refusing to leave until the Punjab was autonomous. On 3 June 1984, Indira Gandhi launched Operation Blue Star in which the army broke into the temple complex in an attempt to remove the Sikhs. Bhindranwale and 1,000 Sikhs died during the ensuing action.

On 31 October, 1984, in revenge for Operation Blue Star, two of Indira Gandhi's Sikh bodyguards, Beant Singh (1950-1984) and Satwant Singh (1962-89) shot her dead in the garden of the Prime Minister's residence in New Delhi. In anti-Sikh riots following the assassination, a million Sikhs were displaced and 3,000 lost their lives.

Rajiv Gandhi was sworn in as prime minister and immediately announced elections. During campaigning, he tried to fight the appeal of nationalist groupings such as the newly formed Bharatiya Janata Party (BJP). Meanwhile, he refused to criticise or distance himself from the right-wing Hindu nationalist and paramilitary party, the Rashtriya Swayamsevak Sangh (RSS). His campaign played very much to the fear that Hindus had of Sikh militants and to a desire for stability. Congress took 404 of the 514 seats in the Lok Sabha.

Rajiv Gandhi

Gandhi devoted his first few months in power to bringing an end to the regional conflicts in Assam, the Punjab and in the tribal state of Mizoram in the northwest of the country. He moved away from the socialist tendencies and government planning ethos of his grandfather Nehru and put his faith in free market thinking and technocratic expertise. Indians began to buy computers, bigger televisions and VCRs after he loosened the rules on licensing and permits. In the 1980s, the Indian economy grew, the growth derived from industry. Some said it was the reward for greater investment in infrastructure that Nehru had begun while others suggested it came from the growth of the Indian middle class who were consuming more.

Soon, however, the regional problems re-surfaced. Troops had to be sent into Assam in 1990 to stop ongoing violence and Sikh terrorists launched attacks in Haryana, Rajasthan, Uttar Pradesh and New Delhi. By 1987 an emergency had been declared in the Punjab and, from 1987 until 1990, Indian troops fought the militant Sri Lankan organisation, the Tamil Tigers, as a peacekeeping force brought in by the Sri Lankan government.

After a campaign that focused on corruption Gandhi's Congress lost four out of six states in the 1988 state elections and in the general election of the following year Congress lost its majority. Vishwanath Pratap Singh (1931-2008), Gandhi's former defence minister, who had made damaging accusations about corruption in the government, won a majority with his Janata Dal Party.

The 'Other Backward Classes'

Janata Dal was a coalition of small socialist and peasant-supporting groupings whose objective was to improve the lot of lower-caste communities. Singh wanted to implement the recommendations of the 1980 Mandal Commission that had considered reserved seats and quotas in order to redress caste discrimination. It was not the first time that politicians had tried to help poor communities – 'Other Backward Classes', or OBCs – who were neither Untouchable nor tribal. The Commission identified 3,248 castes or communities of people. They represented 52.4 per cent of the population, a staggering 350 million. These people would be provided with preferential treatment or positive discrimination that, it was hoped, would improve their living conditions and social prospects. Singh announced the implementation of the Mandal Commission in 1990, ten years after it had sat. Twenty-seven per cent of all government jobs would be reserved for OBCs. The prime minister said: 'We want to give an effective [voice] here in the power structure and running of the country to the depressed, downtrodden and backward people.'

There was a great deal of opposition to the move and shockingly around 300 young higher-caste people tried to kill themselves in protest. After legal battles, the recommendations were finally implemented in 1993, but by then the Indian economy was on the road to a dramatic recovery. The private sector began to provide fabulous opportunities for upper-caste Indians and opposition to the positive discrimination in favour of OBCs faded.

Another Gandhi Assassination

V.P. Singh resigned as prime minister in November 1990, replaced briefly by Chandra Shekhar (1927-2007) before elections the following year. On 21 May 1991, Rajiv Gandhi was campaigning in Sriperumbudur, a village about 25 miles from Chennai when a woman, Thenmozhi Rajaratnam (?-1991) greeted him and bent down to touch his feet. At that moment, she detonated a belt filled with explosives hidden beneath her dress. Gandhi and his assassin were killed instantly and at least 14 other people died. It is believed Gandhi's murderer was a member of the Sri Lankan Tamil Tigers who had decided to eliminate him because he had said in an interview that, were he to be elected prime minister, he would send the Indian Peace Keeping Force back into Sri Lanka to disarm the Tamil Tigers.

For the first time in its history, Congress found itself without a member of the Nehru-Gandhi family to inherit the leadership. It was a remarkable fact that Congress had governed India for 40 of the 44 years since independence and for all but two of those years a member of the famous dynasty had led it. But there was change in the air and Congress had lost a great deal of its support during the years of Indira and Rajiv Gandhi. Indian politics was becoming fragmented and region also began to play a part. Coalitions became the norm and the Indian political landscape was an ever-changing one as parties fell apart or merged with others in an endless series of coalitions. Voters demonstrated very little loyalty to parties, most of which had nothing much in the way of an ideology to which people could respond.

Nonetheless, in 1991, Congress still won enough seats in the Lok Sabha elections to form a government, albeit in a coalition in which they were supported by Tamil Nadu's non-Brahmin DMK party, the Muslim League and the Communist Party of India (Marxist). The role of prime minister went to P.V. Narasimha Rao (1921-2004).

In 1991, the Gulf War caused oil prices to rise and this also had an impact on the price of food. Another result of the conflict was that many Indian workers lost their jobs in the Gulf states and were forced to return home to unemployment. The economy was in a bad way and India came close to defaulting on its international debt. The new finance minister was the economist Manmohan Singh (b. 1932) who made severe cuts in government spending and, in return for a loan of several billion dollars from the International Monetary Fund, devalued the rupee. He sought foreign investors, making it easier for them to invest in India. The immediate effects of these initiatives — unemployment and a rise in inflation — damaged the government but five years later India was in the middle of an economic miracle. There was a huge amount of foreign investment and foreign business flocked to the country. Inflation fell and the middle class prospered. The gap between rich and poor only widened, however.

Chapter Thirteen

India in the Twenty-First Century

In 1947 at independence, India was still largely agricultural but by the twenty-first century it enjoyed a mixed economy. Agriculture played a large part but people were increasingly living in an urban environment. In 1881, less than 10 per cent of the population lived in towns and cities but that figure has now increased to around 28 per cent, and the decade from 1991 to 2001 saw mass migration from the countryside to urban environments. There are now 27 cities in India with a population of more than a million. Modern India is globally connected and many of the old distinctions have disappeared. As one observer has noted, the large Indian middle class is now as likely to define itself by the size of its television or what model mobile phone it uses as by its *jati* or *varna* classification. Culturally, new modes of expression arrived in the form of the internet and satellite technology that allow Indians to express themselves regionally or locally as well as nationally.

India is the world's second most populous nation, the population having grown rapidly since the 1920s when inoculations, new medicines and better public hygiene helped people to live longer. The birth rate began to exceed the death rate. The decades since independence, however, have shown the greatest increase in population. In 1951 it stood at just over 366 million but the billionth Indian was born in May 2000 and, by May 2016, it had risen to 1.3 billion. By 2022, it is reckoned, India will overtake China to become the world's most populous nation. India is a young nation. More than 50 per cent of the population is under 25 and more than 65 per cent is under 35. It has been estimated that by 2020 the average age for an Indian will be 29, while for the Chinese it will be 37 and for Japan 48. And it is an ethnically complex nation with more than 2,000 ethnic groups, every major religion and numerous languages.

In the 27 cities with populations of more than a million, the gap between rich and poor is evident, and one in four is a slum-dweller. In 2001, more than half of Mumbai's inhabitants lived in slums.

Towards the New Century

Many Hindus believe that Rama was born in the city of Ayodhya. Some even insist that the site of the Babri Masjid mosque represents the exact spot. This structure, built in 1528-1529, is said by some to have replaced a Hindu structure that had been erected to mark the birthplace. Disputes over the site began in the nineteenth century and, when the mosque was demolished in December 1992 by militant Hindu nationalist groups, riots between Hindus and Muslims erupted all over India which resulted in the deaths of more than 2,000 people. An investigation blamed a number of people including the leaders of the right-wing Bharatiya Janata Party (BJP), the Rashtriya Swayamsevak Sangh (RSS) and the Vishva Hindu Parishad (VHP) for the demolition. Nonetheless, the BJP came to power in 1998 and 1999 as the lead party in coalition governments, helped into office by upper-caste Hindus from towns and cities.

The BJP won the election of 1996 but because of its aggressively nationalist stance – 'Hindutva', or 'Hinduness' –

it was unable to find partners with whom to form a coalition. Instead, Janata Dal leader H D Deve Gowda (b. 1933) became prime minister, his coalition featuring the United Front and 13 left-leaning regional and low-caste parties. He lasted only ten months, forced out by Congress (I) and replaced by the little-known Inder Kumar Gujral (b. 1919). His was the fourth coalition government of the year but it too fell in a scandal over funding. The BJP won the election of 1998, managing to form a governing coalition. Atal Bihari Vajpayee (b. 1924) was prime minister of India until 2004, the BJP having by this time abandoned its Hindutva philosophy and gained a constituency of both upper-caste Hindus and dominant non-OBC Hindu peasant castes. He was India's tenth prime minister and the first from outside Congress to serve a full five-year term.

Conflicts and Threats

In 1999, Vajpayee had to deal with another conflict with Pakistan – the Kargil War in the Kargil district of Kashmir. The cause was the infiltration of Pakistani soldiers across the Line of Control (LOC) that marked the frontier between the two countries. Several thousand soldiers from both sides died in the fighting which ended with the withdrawal of the Pakistanis who were facing international condemnation for their intrusion into Indian territory.

Natural disasters continue to blight the subcontinent. The 2004 Boxing Day Tsunami struck Andhra Pradesh, Tamil Nadu and Kerala, killed 18,000, and displaced 65,000, and an earthquake in Kashmir killed 79,000 the following year.

India faces a number of threats. Manmohan Singh described the Naxalite-Maoist rebels as 'India's greatest internal security challenge'. This conflict began after the formation of the

Communist Party of India (Maoist) group in 2004 and it has now spread over a huge area that is composed of almost half of India's states. In 2013, 24 leaders of the Indian National Congress died in an attack by around 250 Naxalite-Maoist rebels in Darbha Valley in Chhattisgarh.

The world was horrified by the Mumbai attacks of November 2008 that killed 168 people. Twelve coordinated shooting and bombing attacks were carried out over four days by ten members of the Pakistani Islamic militant organisation Lashkar-e-Taiba. These incidents sent shockwaves through Indian society and evoked global condemnation. This was the latest of a number of terrorist attacks in Mumbai. In 1993, 257 people died when 13 bombs were exploded in protest at the demolition of the Babri Mosque. Ten died in March 2003, when a bomb exploded on a train the day following the tenth anniversary of the 1993 incident, and a further 44 died in August of that year when bombs went off in South Mumbai. Seven bombs on 11 July 2006 killed 209 people.

Confrontation with Pakistan over Kashmir is a constant threat. A stand-off between the two countries occurred in 2001 to 2002 when there was a military build-up on both sides of the border after a terrorist attack on the Indian Parliament on 13 December 2001 and one on the Indian Legislative Assembly on 1 October the same year. The Pakistani Islamic militant groups Lashkar-e-Taiba and Jaish-e-Mohammad were blamed. India claimed that they were backed by Pakistan's intelligence agency, the ISI, but Pakistan denied this. There were fears of a nuclear confrontation between the two as in recent years both had successfully detonated nuclear devices but the tensions were alleviated by international diplomatic intervention. In October 2002, the troops massing on either side of the border were withdrawn.

Politics

In the election of 2004, the BJP's support fell away and, after eight years out of office, Congress returned to power in a coalition named the United Progressive Alliance. This time, it seemed, the power to change governments lay in the hands of rural voters – the poor, the Untouchables and the OBCs.

After Rajiv Gandhi's wife, Sonia – president of Congress – declined the offer of the premiership, Manmohan Singh became the first Sikh and the first non-Hindu to be prime minister. He persisted with policies of liberalisation of the economy but the socialists and communists in his coalition stopped some other initiatives, such as privatisation. Efforts to improve the living conditions of the poor continued and the government announced India's biggest-ever rural jobs plan, aiming to raise 60 million families out of poverty.

In 2007, India elected its first woman president, Pratibha Patil (b. 1934), former governor of Rajasthan, but a long-time associate of the Gandhi family.

In 2009, BJP's support diminished still further and it appeared that India's prosperity was more important to voters than Hindu nationalism. The United Progressive Alliance won a majority with Congress taking the majority of the seats. Once again, however, there were allegations of corruption.

The Return of BJP

In India's sixteenth general election since independence, held in early 2014, the issues were inflation, unemployment, the economy, corruption, religion and terrorism. The Bharatiya Janata Party made a dramatic comeback, as part of the National Democratic Alliance, a centre-right coalition. The BJP won

282 seats – 51.9 per cent – and the right to form the largest majority government since 1984. It was also the first time since that election that a party had won enough seats to form a government without any other party's support. Congress's United Progressive Alliance won only 58 seats, representing the worst-ever performance by Congress in an election. As a result, India remains without an official opposition party as to become the opposition a party must have 10 per cent of the seats in the Lok Sabha and Congress does not have this number. The Chief Minister of Gujarat, Narendra Modi (b. 1950), a Hindu nationalist and described by one commentator as 'one of contemporary India's most controversial and divisive politicians', became prime minister.

India Today

Modi, prime minister of India since 2014, is the former Chief Minister of Gujarat, and was elected on a reform agenda. He heads a government with a neo-liberal take on the economy. It has fostered direct foreign investment in India and has raised expenditure on the country's infrastructure, increasing access to high-speed internet in rural areas, for example. He has also reduced spending on education, health and social welfare and has pushed for a more efficient bureaucracy. Corporate tax has been lowered and wealth tax abolished. Modi has scrapped many of India's employment laws, making it more difficult for workers to form trade unions and rendering it easier for employers to hire and fire. These reforms brought strong opposition and a general strike by most of the country's major unions took place in September 2015. He scrapped India's 65-year-old Planning Commission with its arcane bureaucracy which he claims was stifling growth, replacing it with a new National Institution for

Transforming India. Rather than imposing five-year plans with rigid economic targets as the Planning Commission did, the NITI will act as a think-tank or forum and will offer greater involvement for the regions. Modi has said that it would have a 'pro-people, pro-active and participative development agenda'.

At the start of 2016, India was the world's fastest-growing economy but there has been a significant slow-down. This was exacerbated by a surprising decision in November 2016 when the government scrapped high denomination bank notes. 500 and 1,000 rupee notes were withdrawn from circulation in order to curb counterfeiting – some of which funds terrorism – and to wrong-foot those who had, over the years, hoarded cash on which no tax had been paid. It is estimated that the 'black economy' and counterfeiting account for between 20 and 25 per cent of an Indian economy of which 90 per cent is cash. Eighty-six per cent of the cash in circulation became immediately worthless, leading to turmoil with protests throughout India. Immediately after the announcement, banks across the country had to deal with serious shortages of cash and there were not enough 100, 50, 20 and 10 rupee notes to satisfy demand. This had a serious detrimental effect on many small businesses, farmers and on transportation. To exchange the notes meant long queues at the banks and several deaths have been linked to the rush to exchange banknotes.

It remains to be seen whether Modi's radical steps to create a modern India where corruption, counterfeiting and terrorism are things of the past will be enough to make a difference. However, this prime minister, who dominates Indian politics in a way that has not been seen in decades, seems determined to drag the world's largest democracy kicking and screaming into the twenty-first century.

Bibliography

Keay, John, *India: A History*, Revised Edition, Harper Press, London, 2010

Kulke, H. and Rothermund, D., *A History of India*, Routledge & Kegan Paul, London, 1990

Stein, Burton, *A History of India*, Blackwell, Oxford, 1998

Wolpert, S., *A New History of India*, OUP, Oxford, 2008

Wood, Michael, *The Story of India*, BBC Books, London, 2007

Index

INDEX

INDEX

INDEX

INDEX

INDEX

INDEX

INDEX